Also by Wayne Koestenbaum

Double Talk: The Erotics of Male Literary Collaboration

Ode to Anna Moffo and Other Poems

The Queen's Throat: Opera, Homosexuality, and the
    Mystery of Desire

Rhapsodies of a Repeat Offender

Jackie Under My Skin: Interpreting an Icon

The Milk of Inquiry

Cleavage: Essays on Sex, Stars, and Aesthetics

Andy Warhol

Model Homes

Moira Orfei in Aigues-Mortes

Best-Selling Jewish Porn Films

Hotel Theory

Humiliation

Blue Stranger with Mosaic Background

The Anatomy of Harpo Marx

My 1980s & Other Essays

The Pink Trance Notebooks

The
Pink
Note

Nightboat Books

Wayne Koestenbaum

Trance books

ISBN 978-1-937658-40-3

Designed and composed by Quemadura
Text set in Akzidenz and Didot

Cataloging-in-publication date is available
from the Library of Congress

Distributed by
University Press of New England
One Court Street
Lebanon, NH 03766
www.upne.com

Nightboat Books
New York
www.nightboat.org

for Steven Marchetti

Contents

Trance Notebook #1

[I believe in ruin]   1

Trance Notebook #2

[nerdy questions about exact pitch]   15

Trance Notebook #3

[a testicle descends, but a lark ascends]   28

Trance Notebook #4

[the table doesn't have genitals]   39

Trance Notebook #5

["father" a category almost leviathan]   49

Trance Notebook #6

[family birthmarks surgically removed]   59

Trance Notebook #7

[the shame somersault]   70

Trance Notebook #8

[the erotic father]   79

Trance Notebook #9

[eye drops in a dirty negligee]   85

Trance Notebook #10

[a Marschallin moment in the vanity mirror] 92

Trance Notebook #11

[the nearby succulence of fag ideation] 100

Trance Notebook #12

[fruit binge] 110

Trance Notebook #13

[shaving errors on Perry Street] 122

Trance Notebook #14

[cut it up and then project it] 134

Trance Notebook #15

[the opposite of Tupperware] 145

Trance Notebook #16

[nights illuminated by imperishable clutter] 157

Trance Notebook #17

[the lake and the kink] 171

Trance Notebook #18

[desire demands specialization] 181

Trance Notebook #19

[saloon Jews hijacked the known] 191

Trance Notebook #20

[self-slaughter and poppies]   **203**

Trance Notebook #21

[surreptitious nookie with a large astronaut]   **216**

Trance Notebook #22

[ultramarine has a pocky charisma]   **231**

Trance Notebook #23

[alabaster concussive effect of stillbirth]   **249**

Trance Notebook #24

[naked sailor confronting his Laocoön identity]   **265**

Trance Notebook #25

*[choose grope partners among the
Eddie Fishers and Tony Curtises]*   **274**

Trance Notebook #26

[jade plant phallus lopped off]   **284**

Trance Notebook #27

[nostalgia for the wooden nipple era]   **294**

Trance Notebook #28

[agape gape grape]   **305**

Trance Notebook #29

*[shopworn Cassandra towels in requiem
half-moon]* 316

Trance Notebook #30

[dribble cloth disguised as fashion statement] 329

Trance Notebook #31

[like a camp counselor or a hurricane] 339

Trance Notebook #32

[blow job cut through with lime tenderness] 350

Trance Notebook #33

[I decided not to keep up with the death drive] 360

Trance Notebook #34

[the word she picks for comfort, "hernia"] 376

The Pink Trance Notebooks

Trance Notebook #1

[I believe in ruin]

virgin writing
random crushes—
that guy born
in Israel or
Palestine (today
is Palestine's
birthday)

—————

which Palestine?
Palestine is ambiguous

—————

                    I
believe in ruin

—————

strangely ruined
by the collapse of
my voice

———

butt-fucked—
I meant to say
bullet-wounded
(earlier I mentioned
Robert Kennedy)

———

disgust—wishing
to throw this book
away before I
even begin writing it—

———

not proceeding
intentionally—instead,
using oil pastels carelessly

———

his finger repeatedly
in my ass—

———

a new
career as bottom?

———————

incarcerated
and foul?

———————

an enemy
of speed?

———————

am I
the deadly
virus responsible for the
collapse of my mother's
viability?

———————

or some such
hyperbole

———————

second- or third-
hand smoke of my putative
prowess—an assertion

I surround with
as much irony as I can
muster

———————

convince
exigent witnesses that my
attackers are wrong—
impossible task!

———————

waiting for re-
installation of the lost
crown—

———————

Q-tip
exercises in mad
utterance—

———————

to make sure my penis
aims only in one
direction

———————

for
three hours

_____

        at the
speed of light

_____

    his cock
rather large and never
hard (how can someone
avoid erection for three
hours?)

_____

and I'm not bringing
this up for the sake of
literary filigree

_____

    the
girl around the block
whose father died
recognized me,

she had a folk-rock
consanguinity with my
darker inclinations

———————

orange roses
the color of
dropping acid—

———————

seeing *Barbarella*
for the first time

———————

to keep
alive the synapses,
even if I resemble
a bedbug, or
two abstract squares
of rusticated stucco

———————

a considerable omission
on her upper lip, in
addition to arthritis

————

a Giacometti sculpture—
The Invisible
Object

————

       fellated
under an apple tree
that gave only crab
apples we
assumed were quinces—
stunted, ugly, hard,
and not numerous

————

watery identification
and willed mental
illness? hermaphrodite?

————

baggy flap of skin
behind each shoulder?

————

rotten
rabbit teeth

———————

awful canal of
my face, Anne
Frank gutter—

———————

a way
to escape it—
bubbles

———————

exceed in complexity
Michelangelo's Laurentian
library, cold gray
steps in 1985

———————

and I've seen them
only once, in 1985

———————

Stephen
Baldwin today
incarcerated as a
felon for not paying
taxes—

_____

Fauré's song "Les Roses
d'Ispahan"—all roses
are second-rate

_____

Lebanese guy
showered with
curtain drawn not
merely because he's
a psychiatrist—but
being a psychiatrist
contributed to his
reluctance to let
me see his cock and
ass—

_____

horizon lines
in nude photographs
often in the
spirit of post-
Hiroshima traumatized
calm?

_____

time stopped then and
has still not resumed—
when evil erupts, time
stops, and it never
revives, only a
simulacral
time recommences,
but genuine time withers

_____

an absolutely free
and uncondemned speech—

_____

condemnations
exist (or

transpire) within the
blessed space of
the uncondemned—

———————

The Killing of Sister George
should have been a
larger landmark in
my childhood—
why did Sister George
go unrecognized in my
orisons?

———————

a Seville orange
reeks of my father—
its sharpness, its
vulnerability to being
squeezed

———————

I
heard Anna Moffo's
1969 (infamous)

mad scene—in
severely compromised
voice—and found
it enthralling

_____

dreamt that M_____
stood behind me (ambush)
and pressed into my
rear end—as if she
were butt-fucking me—
and in the dream her
mental illness was
established as factual—

_____

　　　　we
sat together in a
yoga space—
ersatz, fraudulent,
connected to a failed
painter, a charlatan—

_____

my father? my
father's mistress?

———————

abstract lines serving
representational ends

———————

lines *not knowing*
they're abstract

———————

lines ending up
abstract because
they're so intently
concentrated on
capturing observed form

———————

"the first
time I heard
the word *glitch*"

———————

odd textures and geometries
painted in quadrants

_____

cadmium blues?
antimony
poisoning?

_____

Van Cliburn died
yesterday—he described
adolescence as "hell"

_____

Susan Howe asked
me for advice on her
scarf, whether or not
to wear it—I said *yes,*
wear it, but make sure
it doesn't conceal
your lovely necklace

Trance Notebook #2

[nerdy questions about exact pitch]

today's the
anniversary of
Pearl Harbor

————

I'll never wear
Fiesta Bisque

————

    I'm
a "super-cool"
stutterer

————

    "dress and
run," jock check,
gym coach's
mustache, his French-
teacher wife, her
teeth, shrill
voice, inability

to teach me colors,
exclamation-point
eyebrows

———————

thunderstorms, black
chunky glasses,
international food
court of 1964

———————

last Sunday's
dying cockroach
my sentimental pet

———————

defiant
personality syndrome?
Cy Twombly book on
my lap—

———————

hair pattern on Cliff's
legs, barbecue
pit near the creek—

———

not
liking Updike's *Midpoint*
is part of my intellectual
history, more important
than never reading
Thucydides

———

an attraction to line,
not because it's phallic,
but because I like it

———

French
kisser near the donut-
shop parking lot and
a used copy of *The
Fox*

———

anonymous
mushroom-head penis
wielder in the Public
Garden, Botticelli
didn't draw you

———————

Christo
wrapped me

———————

balletic
make-out sessions with
plagiarists

———————

"let's
include cocksucking
in our low-key friendly
chats"

———————

I wrote
down every word the
drunk jocks muttered

———————

like a
Sicilian folksong sung
in French translation by
Tino Rossi, 1920

—————

    or blueberry
pancakes soaked in bourbon

—————

    or
a bowl of inedible
toffee suckers

—————

    like a
Contes d'Hoffmann performance
in Nice, 1942—
yes, there were operetta
performances during the war

—————

I thought poop was
Satan—which means
I loved Satan, or
considered him a co-
conspirator, a radio play

—————

a non-
stop figure skater

_____

or forgetting how to
bake chocolate chip
cookies, and choosing
derangement over
daffodils

_____

so I
can violate them
in the clothing store
where I buy a
woman's seersucker
jacket

_____

let me
try on the woman's
Fourth-of-July-patterned jumpsuit

_____

       sell me a clip-on
bow tie or a mock
fringe chapeau worn on
the collarbone—a
new style of "shoulder
hat," a cape to
protect your shoulders
from rain and chill and
to prevent the wearer
from sliding (like
Mickey Mantle) into
a third gender

—————

       now I've
reached the "clinker" zone
of perforated opportunities

—————

       —perforated appurtenances

—————

but then Edith Piaf
suddenly thrilled me

———

a newly
discovered Venezuela, a
view—

———

a *rendre compte*,
a liar on the corner
(thirsty corner) of
23rd and 9th, a gazelle,
a rendezvous chapel

———

(a chaplet of
daisies around my
pleurisy brow)—

———

flirty and lubricated
in medias res

———

he mentioned
La forza del destino as

touchstone, and I
asked repeated nerdy
questions about exact
pitch (there's no such
thing as exact pitch)

———————

translate
13 French compositions
into German and
distribute them as
pity leaflets in Dresden—

———————

and the clinking
of fragile petals

———————

your kerchief
and your early death
a Beethoven keepsake—
like Steinhof
church atop the
schizophrenic hill

———————

    we claimed
old age as our icy
mirror, our Bruegel

———————

I may be the
cousin of Maya
Deren but I
live in Chile among
refugees of a
God That Failed psycho-
analysis

———————

     my
brutalist tutor, my
Meneghini

———————

    j'ai
besoin de vous he
sentimentally told his
Russian mistress, O

Tuscan olive oil, O
cyanide, O tanned
drill team thigh of
a perseverator, O
wig of the pale
cancer death of the
scarlet ibis, bad
short story, bad
collaborationist

———————

I didn't know Matisse
was also a sculptor

———————

like a Julie London
impersonator, the hum
of the malfunctioning
heater

———————

he went to San José
State College, where my
father taught—

_____

one of
those wife-beaters I
tend to fall in love with

_____

thank you
for smashing my
Sondheim LPs

_____

like a sucked-on
Life Saver, an epidural

_____

little
garbage disposal,
little male-pattern baldness

_____

I smell
cookies baking—an
immodest proposal,
an accusation shaped

like a children's picture
book based on Cultural
Revolution purges, dear Father

_____

it shouldn't have
provoked disgust,
but it did

_____

wonder why my right
hand (murderer
drowned in malmsey
butt) is sweaty

Trance Notebook #3

[a testicle descends, but a lark ascends]

a foetid
pool of Anadyomene images—

————

—don't confuse self-
deprecation with "unacknowledged
legislators" transport—

————

your naked
shoulders, the girlie raw
material of lieder—

————

(cave paintings and trills)

————

arm lying
dead on the wheelchair
ledge—

————————

      clairvoyance of our
anus, its
(somber) solitude,
hemiola—not
the children's hospital
near San Francisco State
University

————————

      no one
becomes a German citizen
because of breeze or jazz,
no one becomes a German
citizen overnight—no
one becomes Mado Robin
overnight, or any dead
legend—

————————

Melville's pervy *Pierre,*
subject of my 2001 reveries—

————————

guillotine revolutionaries and
their quadrille-dreaming
wives—not all
revolutionaries are husbands—

—————

no reason I shouldn't
have a crush on Jesus
or picture his pierced
flayed abdomen

—————

his nipples
in recession

—————

I frequent the Tinker's
Damn, an atopical
gay bar also patronized
by Tiny Tim and
Miss Vicki

—————

my shame is one-size-
fits-all, like a white
parka from Target

———————

     afraid of
Debussy and stomach
flu—

———————

the relationship between
early impressionism and
intestinal bugs

———————

Jean Harris, who
murdered the Diet Doctor,
died today—

———————

it ODs on indexicality

———————

—a nightingale
without a onesie is a
venereal "state of
exception"

———————

lollipops were *de
rigueur* when boys'
testicles were undescended—
a testicle descends, but
a lark ascends

———————

Wilhelm
Reich and other Radical
Faerie technicians of the
sacred perineum, the
ligament between the wolf
and the regurgitator—

———————

illness alters aesthetic
judgments—

———————

sunsets are sentimental
propaganda tools, yet
every night a sunset
makes a threepenny-opera
hooker out of me—
I expand like an
accordion before it's had
a chance to be
a scarlet pimpernel—

—————

            —all
chapels are identical when
perceived by the belly button
of the faithful—

—————

        I thought
the phone call meant
my mother had died,
but he left no
message, and if she'd
died, wouldn't he
have left a message
saying "she died"?

—————

the redheaded Israeli-
Austrian trainer strained
my neck by suggesting
a perverse free-weight
hamstring-glute exercise

—————

　　　　he urges me
to apply for German
citizenship

—————

　　vaginas are
higher and more tilted
than I'd realized

—————

　　　　the area by
the bushes in elementary
school (Lassen Drive?)
seemed the location of a
dead body

—————

these sentences
lead to Switzerland, the Klee
asylum, recovery, *Ash
Wednesday,* plastic surgery,
doomed nose jobs,
Joan Rivers flirting
with my boyfriend in
cafeteria and ignoring me

_____

this activity
represents a symptom of
neurological damage

_____

Ingres painted a peacock
feather, though the man
who wrote the Ingres
book on which I'm leaning
is dead

_____

my mother (I think)
telephoned, and my
heart stopped—

————————

I make nonsense sounds
because I pretend I
live in a toaster—
I pretend I'm a Pop-Tart—

————————

   —peevishness
isn't the same as
a poetic credo—
and yet I assert
crabbiness and
grandiosity as a
modernist torch—

————————

   my mother's
bowels are always a
part of my consciousness,
and that's why I
flee consciousness,
because I don't
want to be a tenant
of my mother's bowels—

———

a strange choice for
Orthodox Jews in
search of pomegranates

———

     like Courbet
origin-of-the-world
bagel-and-cream-cheese
concession stands on
8th Avenue

———

my pockets are filled
with lumpy stars—
fetal
constellations

———

like Jim Nabors with
a morning woody—
greeting his new roommate,
Jerry Seinfeld—
Jerry's wearing his
Mame costume—

———————

I'm
trying to avoid a
crevice—or abyss—
in the middle of my
mother's bed,
where she awaits my
response, though she
doesn't always remember
who I am—

———————

—she always
remembers that I am
a cardboard doll, a
St. Francis of Assisi loser fetish

Trance Notebook #4

[the table doesn't have genitals]

        aggressions, pointillist
or grisaille

––––––––––

        chickens
called my bones
"bird-like," meaning not
a *Mandate* or *Inches*
centerfold

––––––––––

pianist onanist,
monochrome practitioner

––––––––––

I could draw your leg
or I could *cook*
your leg

––––––––––

my purple pants have
red crayon stains

———————

your lips wiggle when you
read Gide

———————

male philosopher
as seafood aspic

———————

nostalgic
for H.D., for Mina
Loy, for Samantha in
Bewitched, for *Amahl
and the Night Visitors*—
a performance interrupted
by necking sophomores

———————

he plays
ukulele by the river
at sunset

—————

garbage bags go flap or
smack like
prayer flags

—————

"crystalline," a word
I'll never use

—————

I shocked the James
Taylor lookalike with
my badly timed hard-on

—————

　　　end my career
before *Torn Curtain*

—————

Wursthaus, where we
ate (out of false nostalgia)
in 1976

—————

the guy whose gallery
I tried to visit was sick

———————

the guys
who flirt with me
tend to be diseased

———————

a revenge
fantasy I worked up
while watching *The
Flintstones*

———————

lust
for Barney's shave-
needing jaw

———————

each day a new Bible
verse to use as
purgative

———————

          my
grandmother at the
Art Deco fair in
Paris, 1925—
posing as
a *grisette*

—————

forward motion is
antithetical to
spiritual transport

—————

I don't want to regain
consciousness—the
Swan Lake school of
euthanasia, permanent
somnolence,
IV drip
Valhalla

—————

everything
I am is damned—

————————

   describe
a ricotta tart

————————

   three-
dimensionalizing my
captivity, treating it
like a *Glass Menagerie*
system of symbolic
equivalences

————————

   the table
is cream-colored and
squat

————————

   the table
doesn't have genitals

————————

how happy the table
must be, to live

without sexual
identity, sitting
in its foretold place,
like Lot, a good
servant of the state

———————

      mornings
when I skipped synagogue
and lay in bed and watched
Flower Drum Song
as a suicidal plunge
away from responsibilities

———————

      my likeness to
Erda

———————

chugging Red Bull in
Lausanne

———————

chew the
inside of my cheek
like a betel nut
pacifier

———————

heal his anus,
mortify it and then
un-mortify it

———————

don't try those
Buster Keaton tactics
on me—please remove
the word "genial"
from your vocabulary

———————

interludes
of trance, when
my blood flows
topaz

———————

Kim Novak's final
film should have
co-starred Anna Karina
in a *tzigane* mode—

————————

open your temple
for me to pour some
lumen into its
teak aperture—

————————

redwood
or eucalyptus—
aromas of my
rage

————————

the guy who
tried to sell me a
blue cardigan sweater
flashed his cock's
flat head—like
a tepid rattlesnake—

———————

I memorized the vista—
what else was I
supposed to do with it?

———————

       we
watched the Grieg piano
concerto octaves
(cadenza) from the
perspective of the soloist's
inebriated mother, or else
her neighbor, whose
lawn was dying—

———————

I'm the gardener,
I'm guilty of
its death by drought

Trance Notebook #5

["father" a category almost leviathan]

        pretend *La Rondine*
is playing, Leigh Bowery
singing Magda,
light fog draping the fake
city in which I live,
wastrel, procrastinator

————

        he tried to molest me
by pouring gay-pride
water in my washing
machine

————

        I said
"I'm not fond of
sublimation"

————

au fond
at bottom

_____

to make amends for
liquid violence

_____

    potentially
rioting crowds gathered
outside our window

_____

a violation I was
supposed to enjoy

_____

"they're part of a
Fellini movie," I said

_____

    sitting
beside an heiress

_____

later I'd pretend to
covet a peanut

butter and jelly sandwich
served by her famous mother

———————

"are you allowed
to enter your famous
mother's bedroom?
does she hobnob
with Boston priests
indicted as child molesters?"

———————

I said
(to the child psychologist)
"your eyes," meaning "I'm
in love with your eyes,"
not certain I was
actually in love with his
eyes, afraid
I was pouring rapture
in a profitless void

———————

to appear
rich, I ate

honey-glazed pig's trotters
in his admiring presence

—————

writing
is like impaling myself
with a two-foot-long
pronged dildo—for
educational purposes

—————

to become an
expert on Benjamin
Franklin's promiscuity

—————

all his patients were
acting out *Casablanca*—
a group therapy theatrical

—————

"Picasso" is an
alias the child
psychologist assumes when

overcome by fear
of nuclear weapons

———————

it's possible to be
swaddled by stillness and
then (one moment later) to
be *attacked* by stillness

———————

diapers are agents
of aggression

———————

the girl threw up after the party
because her philosopher father
gave her fifty bucks to buy books
(*The Senses of Walden* her first choice)

———————

the philosopher's clubfoot son
stretched out his leg in morning light—

———————

not because he loved Spinoza
but because the health-food craze
(ubiquity of apple
juice) made "father"
a category almost leviathan
in its ability to wrap
a nation in thrall

_____

searching for a teacher
(aware that no
teacher will suffice)

_____

    my father
persuaded the perfect
piano teacher to take me on,
despite her reluctance

_____

"ambushed," I murmured,
imitating Isabelle Huppert
as psychopathic postal worker

———————

we ruined
the experiment, we loved
saying "ruin"

———————

looking for a
pharmacy on Blvd
St-Germain—searching
for over-the-counter birth
control pills we'd use
"off-label" as baldness remedies

———————

I made a film
(Warhol-style) of the child
psychologist and me
orally grappling

———————

IBM and the Holocaust
a book on our shelf

———————

the dog
invited me to a Wagner concert

————————

I flirted with the dog
by begging for a lavatory

————————

my archaisms
alienated the dog

————————

to save face, I
lied to the dog and fled in a cab

————————

if I quit
my dog-oriented activities
I'd be left with nothing—

————————

the dog despised
my filial piety—

————————

his small paws
freakishly unmodulated

_____

the dog was an artist
of atmospheres,
but "atmosphere," too,
was a box, a cage

_____

      Bourgogne Aligoté
or Muscadet, either is
acceptable, the snob-dog
silently indicated—

_____

he specialized in
interstitial emotions

_____

he specialized in over-
articulating interstitial emotions

_____

trying to name
nature's varieties, Linnaeus
grew tongue-tied and
taxonomically confused,
losing the ability to
reign over categories
that were his namesake

Trance Notebook #6

[family birthmarks surgically removed]

dream: crazy naked woman
squatted in my car's back seat,
if it indeed was mine—

————————

afraid we'd smell
each other's privates

————————

faux pas: I praised
"authorship" as gold standard

————————

nude car-squatter
furiously working on a
musical composition—

————————

my car an old jalopy
my grandparents
drove in the 1940s

————

Deanna Durbin died today,
91 years old

————

toilet paper stuck to patent-leather
pump sole of pianist
returning from lavatory

————

éclatant effect of
sudden insight—
impossible to explain
éclatant to you

————

eagerness of Naples
yellow to blend with red

————

Taylor Mead died, 88

————

eagerness of burnt
umber to blend with red

———————

masking tape is
the answer
to compositional crisis

———————

dream: Marcel Duchamp
lay back in a fancy
skirt and kicked legs
in the air

———————

Duchamp was finally
on my side, but perhaps
he'd become unreliable
and lost his clout

———————

I lacked compassion
for the stick figure—

———————

two hugs near toilet
despite paint-smeared shirt—

———————

crying baby boy, glad
recipient of new diapers,
wears cinnabar
tennies and is probably
a girl

_____

     —low
steamy balls of
yachting architect,
cuddly Jew

_____

a leopard grazed upon the river green
a leopard confused about his identity
a leopard not quite compos mentis

_____

the composer of hooker ditties wet the bed
the composer of hooker ditties read Balzac instead
of eating processed cheese

_____

unable to digest a Zwieback cookie

———————

       macaroni and cheese,
take me seriously, play
banjo as Messiaen played
trilling birds—

———————

       the composer concentrating,
stalag prisoner revered
by starlings, matter's librarians

———————

       always a cumulus cloud over
Andean fixities, mountains
no mother blessed

———————

fatigue of mountain
no one will anthropomorphize or love

———————

our incapacity to understand
Lorca's green

———————

Thanksgiving
mother in Poetry Center San
José bathroom
a dream certainty

————————

he has a hairy wrist or
fails to acquire
a hairy wrist

————————

memory of fraternal psycho-
tropic hosanna-epistle

————————

leaden and orange
cantaloupe and "bottom
nature" wish
to refrain from striving

————————

cloudless hills with forest dots,
timber freckles

————————

her hand reaching backward to
rhapsodize me

———————

architect toilet-trained
at eight months, toilet
training no Orpheus described

———————

cahiers Valéry sought
to replace and consummate art—
smudges in his journal
the best part

———————

intruding asemic lines
in midst of semes—

———————

      her scrawl,
her breathing—
tanks of oxygen

———————

         her undigested
food, her gray skin tone

————

super-handsome Dutch
pale blue-eyed
hotel lobby
clerk paying attention
to tall blond girl
now looks briefly at me

————

dream: nude Belgian model
or his equivalent
set fire to my couch
by making lesbian love on it—

————

hard-on at Starbucks
in response to Indian guy ordering
caramel ribbon swirl

————

its edge uneven,
corrugated—

————————

    a theme
park (Faneuil Hall) version
of Anne Frank's secret annex?

————————

family birthmarks
surgically removed—
we are always removing
our birthmarks—

————————

           my
mother's leg, the uncovered
one last night, was
not the birthmarked leg—

————————

while Sisyphus watched

————————

I have the same amount
of mother I've
always had

————————

amid puppets, my fat
hand a shadow play

————————

genderless philosopher's
Achilles' heel

————————

without a gay bar I'm
dead—

————————

while talking
to my mother
I drew her portrait
again and again

————————

    I miss the
days when I wore
suspenders

————————

     goodbye
Mr. Suspender Man

————————

Mr. Suspender Man
sounds like Annette Funicello
"Mr. Piano Man" bought
secondhand at carnival

————————

not trusting rearview mirror,
father driving away from carnival
turns around to compensate
for blind spot

Trance Notebook #7

[the shame somersault]

I will teach you
how to smile for the
camera

———————

how to compensate
for facial sag

———————

dream: Jayne
Mansfield accused
me of sexual harrassment
though I had no
sexual interest in her

———————

my cactus died—
broke off from its
root and lay like a fallen
soldier on the table

—————

tall man's black and
gray stubble, any
stubble but my own

—————

dream face trembling
with contained anger,
a Jewish man
wearing culottes

—————

the young girl sang
French folksongs
under her breath as
she fastened her hood

—————

poet from Córdoba
gave me this beige
pen, the first ballpoint
I've loved in forty years

—————

the bathroom has many
flaws I won't
enumerate here

_____

does *E. coli* remain on the hands
even after washing with soap?

_____

I sought a quieter
gay bar and he said mockingly
"Do you want a retirement home?"

_____

    we set off
the emergency alarm system
three times at the Goethe Institute

_____

dream: shame somersault:
soprano showed vagina
and then quickly
buttocks while bowing
either in Boston's

Symphony Hall or
Amsterdam's Concertgebouw

_____

    I'm there
to witness it: surrounded
by failure like ermine—

_____

    as a nude
performer, she was a
Gramsci-style "organic
intellectual"—

_____

suddenly the dream
soprano's clothes gone, she
lies flat onstage—

_____

    nude, she can't
leave the auditorium—

_____

she flips around, trying
to escape exposure

—————

flipping
is a tactic we call
the "shame
somersault"—

—————

we see
orifices she
wishes would remain
hidden—now
distended, illumined—

—————

end of "Divinités
du Styx" dream—

—————

"I've
outgrown twink
wiles," he said—

———

roulades I knew before
incapacity overtook me—

———

deaths pile up
without remedy—
Daniel Reich's suicide

———

Maria Tallchief died,
I showed *Firebird*
to my class—

———

now listening to Risë
Stevens's Gluck—
she, too, died this year—

———

        Lorine Niedecker had
a quick, lilting, high voice—
rapid oscillations—speedy
but then islands of drawl—

no indulgence in "bee-loud
glade" tactics—

—————

Hudson died—
he once told me
that a much-
touted young poet
of our acquaintance
had a big dick—
mere supposition—

—————

Schuyler said "one
lousy cigarette"—
I say "one lousy
sandwich"—

—————

Astrid Varnay changed
vocal categories mid-career—
I'm changing
vocal categories

—————

to attempt Tin Pan Alley
paintings with islands
of black gesso like pizza crusts—

_____

survivor eating cold
corn on the cob—
a clever snack—

_____

"three things we didn't
know about Ethel Kennedy"

_____

in our family we
grew up using excessive
amounts of toilet paper—

_____

figure out whether cute
Israeli opera director
is gay and what good
it does me if he is—

_____

survivor still eating
cold corn on the cob,
ends sheathed in foil

Trance Notebook #8

doctor who gave me
meningitis shot makes
lavender and vanilla
soap as hobby
but hasn't heard of linden flowers

—————

the erotic father
erasing me—
the place I'll always choose

—————

to fall in love while
cruising a deathly
neighborhood

—————

the pissing multitude said Lorca
climbing up the rock face

—————

trying to communicate lust
through an intervening wall

—————————

in the sandwich shop
someone said "baguette"—
I misheard it as "faggot"

—————————

ask yet another bartender
whether he wants to model

—————————

"diarrhea from Edy's
mint chocolate chip"
she said in the laundry room—
her disclosure unrequested

—————————

I used the phrase
"hegemony over your heart"
in an email to a student

—————————

she said the color lilac
recurs in Picasso's poetry

―――――――

my mother had a stroke in
February and I began
to paint in September

―――――――

her stroke had no magical
power over my actions

―――――――

spent day affixing
mothball-smelling blue
tape onto watercolor paper

―――――――

a zest to be masochistically
accommodating

―――――――

small paranoid
abstract painting
implies Bette Davis

————

scholar who wrote
about incest
presses his
crotch against mine

————

time to send a flirtatious
message to the swarthy
inaccessible oncologist?

————

dreamt again of
Streisand suddenly
intimate in her house—
afraid of career and
mood vacillations

————

don't pretend that tombs
are cozy

————

no one gave me the script
for *The Wizard of Oz* though
I gladly starred in it—

———————

impetigo—
davening?

———————

chest hair of avant-garde pianist—
my crush not reciprocated
despite repeated hugs

———————

assaulted by burnt
cinammon toast turpitude—
a Frieda Hughes sensation—
anointed yet orphaned—

———————

claustrophobia with curator
who turns out *not* to be
habitué of the Sotadic Zone—

———————

beast, please show me
your new
abdominal
floral tattoo

_____

cicadas, Lambrusco
chirr of
newspaper page
turning, Mendelssohn
songs without words,
Kindertransport, wrinkled
white curtains, periodicity
of dying cicadas—

Trance Notebook #9

[eye drops in a dirty negligee]

put holes
on paper and uncover
only certain words

_____

       don't
use Prussian blue—
only use leftover
Persian rose,
Egyptian violet—

_____

dreamt I pointed
out expensive Chanel
bag to torn-lipped
Teutonic *répétiteur*
with wide awkward
body who'd begun
modeling for *Vogue*

———————

     my quickness
is Klytemnestra but my lower
moods are Persephone—

———————

mother ripped up green
chip stamps, or blue—
which was the first
wound, the first destruction?
did she destroy my blue
chip stamps, or green?

———————

the temple destroyed in
two steps—
green and blue—

———————

I resorted to
blue after green
had been destroyed

———————

green chip stamps
redemption counter
at Sears—

————————

"I love every color
you're wearing"—
I don't love the
wax darkly congregating
in your ear

————————

Klytemnestra's mother,
Leda, flying to Calcutta to
meet a boy I've
been sex-chatting with

————————

in part because of his
bald spot
though bald spots per se
don't turn me on

————————

Paul Lynde (surprise!)
appears in *Beach Blanket Bingo*
with Don Rickles
and Buster Keaton

———————

my mother looking forward to
a burnt hamburger
as a "night on the town"—
the town is Sunnyvale—

———————

pregnant woman in summer
whites at smoke-filled bar

———————

woman with anorexia
at outdoor café on
90-degree day

———————

inexplicable bruise (cellulitis?)
on right leg—
residue of insect murdered
before bed

———————

Dominic's mono
in first grade—
legendary diseases of
my older brother's classmates

———————

collection of scat porn
in contemporary penthouse
resembling a silo
not a popular topic
on NPR

———————

forehead swollen with
fluid—and if that is his
forehead where is his anus?

———————

Tauber singing Lehár,
a tune so sticky
I can't abandon it

———————

she understands fear
of highway driving
en route to mortuary
because she yearns to
moonlight as novelist

_____

envying babies who
live to be 120

_____

Magdalena the nurse
dispenses eye
drops in a dirty
negligee

_____

her eye drops are
Susan Hayward

_____

holding a May 2013
copy of *National
Geographic* just like in
the waiting-room poem

———————

I want to remain
a living vegetable—
my vegetable status
might contain
solid thinking

Trance Notebook #10

[a Marschallin moment in the vanity mirror]

"I have to go to the
bathroom" says a crabby
woman doing crossword puzzles

————————

"Alan, I don't feel good,
I have terrible pains
in my stomach"

————————

"he said there's no way
the tumor could be
outside my stomach"

————————

a Marschallin moment
in the vanity mirror

————————

consoling nature of
male underarm odor

though seventh grade
is the time to learn
how to prevent it

———————

Dostoevsky's anti-Semitism—
disintegrating reason

———————

I used the phrase
"boy prison" in a painting
today imitating Chaim
Soutine's pastry chef

———————

leg and blue underthings
visible when brother
pulls back her blanket

———————

ceramic or porcelain dog
her psychiatrist sent—
transitional object
on TV tray—

———————

      what
do you call a sodomized
horse?

_____

dreamt about Debbie Harry,
candy, Bay Area figurative
artists, dead Ingres

_____

did I have a problem
with excessive masturbation
as a kid?

_____

don't remember
masturbating in kindergarten
though I remember
darkness-at-noon
naps and crushing boredom

_____

      simplicity of
(as Frost might have put it?)

original relation
sought by waterfall

—————

did Stein
rush through life or
slowly ruminate?

—————

is
rumination different
from contemplation?

—————

"Black Rectangles,"
story I wrote in 1981,
opened with a sexual
murder, an attempt
to be noir—

—————

I was reading
John Hawkes, on John
Barth's recommendation

———

listening to Debussy's
Baudelaire songs and
loving them mostly
because of another singer
who sang them—

———

loyalty to a different
record than the record
I'm actually listening to—

———

today I drew a
lizard, dinosaur,
rabbit, baby,
hieroglyphic
auto-da-fé

———

    Viennese coffeehouse
has low tables
well-suited to shrimpy
patrons

———————

    alexandrine
with mellifluously lengthened
third syllable

———————

my face haggard
in eyeglass-store mirror

———————

start painting crucifixions,
a zesty subject

———————

now that the left eye
is clearer I notice
flaws in the right—

———————

that's not James Franco's hard-on
in Paul McCarthy's installation

———————

father can't drive us
to *Music Man* rehearsal so
brother and I take a cab

———————

cabdriver stops,
opens his door, spits
onto the pavement—
are we in danger?

———————

either this is a
nostalgic memory
or it isn't—
a temperature
I can't figure out—

———————

the only boy shrimpier
than me in fifth grade,
John, a mutt,
probably queer

———————

I lug my venery
to Chopin's grave

————————

"hawk a loogie" in
the rich man's ass—
said Catullus?

————————

"she always brings
a gassy vegetable
to potluck suppers"—
so said Sadie, or Pearlie,
my great-aunts, dead—

————————

Goldsteins I hardly knew—
I'm no expert
on their apothegms

Trance Notebook #11

[the nearby succulence of fag ideation]

ordered chambray
pants for mother
and cotton/cashmere hoodie

_____

abstract painter compared
a man's basket
to three squirrels

_____

the music that has chosen you—
haute-nursery
oneiric simplicity

_____

paint self-portraits
on baby clothes—
buy a cheap onesie
and gesso it

_____

should I tattoo my eyebrows
with permanent liner?

————————

Lvov is German-identified—
I needn't be ashamed
of coming from Lvov

————————

I am the love
child of Las Vegas
and Belarus

————————

      cross
out the offensive
piece of cuke under
my tongue

————————

I Could Go On Flossing
was not Judy Garland's final movie—
I Could Go On Flossing
was Rita Hayworth's

nightmare version
of *The Maltese Falcon*

_____

never leave the house
without a toothpick
or else turn my tongue
into a toothpick

_____

begin to remember
everything straight men say

_____

Wasser I said
in French

_____

horror of nothingness
and breeze like Tippi
Hedren feels in *Marnie*
assaulted me before sex

_____

are the phalli in
The Prince Comes
gay porn stars
or straight?

———————

gun moll's insane cackle
in Marimekko caftan

———————

he's
half-Jewish and not
interested in Jewishness
making egregious
appearances in progressive
contemporary art
ergo vegetable dumplings

———————

hairless
arms ignoring me and
listening to music
rather than eating
the nuts I so generously
offered you

———————

    like a psychotic
detective novelist
signing books "much love"
and "life is good"

———————

bought my mother
yoga pants
though she can't walk
and will probably never
again do yoga
except the corpse position
which she does every day
and every night

———————

    on Jerry Lewis
muscular dystrophy telethon
Joan Crawford reads a poem
("The Clumsy, Falling-Down Child")
and professes to be deeply moved

———————

on another TV show
she recites Edna St. Vincent Millay's
"Dirge without Music"
which includes the words "the dull"
and the repeated phrase
"I am *not* resigned"
each time (in Joan's rendition)
said more angrily

———————

Wet One canister made
a hollow clack
as it fell in garbage

———————

give up prose
please give it up
or give up autonomic
hormone surge
of fight or flight—

———————

Barrel of Monkeys
a store-bought
game I played

————————

she looked adopted
(no one can look adopted)

————————

    every baby is
adopted—when the parents
choose not to abandon
or disown the newborn
they are thus adopting
the child, even if
biologically theirs

————————

to quote Grace Slick,
who advised me
once upon a time in
fairyland—

————————

we agree not to
eavesdrop on one another

————————

I write
farm letters, full
of pasture smells—

———————

freckles on
upper faun arm means
he's straight and therefore
not potentially in love
with me though also
a hyacinth

———————

Fata Morgana
we can't see
in the tunnel's dark—

———————

————— is a secret
homophobe, secret
even to himself— he finds
mirthful the eccentric
exhalations of fags—

———————

snide critic can't
thrive without the nearby
succulence of fag
ideation, yet he wants
to exterminate it

_____

I, however, need
the presence of nearby
sexy men to experience
a burst of poetic frenzy

_____

as if this painting
were a dramatic monologue
in the voice of a houseplant
whose repeated, petulant cry
is "I'm not on Facebook"

_____

afraid to touch
the bottom of my suitcase
because I drag it
on wheels through
filthy streets

———————

same distribution of
E. coli on rich street
and poor street, or
maybe there is more
E. coli on rich street?

———————

write a nice poem
about ethics and *E. coli*
for a morally
engaged magazine

Trance Notebook #12

[fruit binge]

punctuation is evil

————————

         straight
couples jogging in the morning—

————————

abrupt untoward and
inappropriate glimpses
of antidote cock

————————

I'm on a fruit binge,
Saturn peach in the
bedroom

————————

        when I didn't
know my gender or
couldn't assume that it

was legible or would be
unproblematically recognized
and authorized by others—

————————

and then at least
once in the airport
I'm called "ma'am"

————————

          gave my
mother a dented
Saturn peach—

————————

          Marty
did ironing for my
mother—"I paid her
50 cents"—

————————

    I help brother
put my mother's paralyzed
hand in its splint to
prevent spasm—

———————

    stranger's eyes
seem willing to meet
mine, though mayhap he's
just curious about how a
Jew with patterned
shirt could write so quickly

———————

my mother's scrawled
words on a yellow pad

———————

"babies look cute in suncaps—
all the baby books said
give your baby an hour or two
of sunshine per day"

———————

    dream:
on a committee with Jorie
Graham, I said that
Dan Graham was a

figure of world historical
importance and should get
the award—Jorie agreed
because, like me, she
relished shortcuts—

_____

    —these sentiments
too coarse for singing onstage—

_____

enhance chaos

_____

    as if it were
a widely known fashion
phenomenon to keep
boots unzipped—

_____

mother looks at me but
doesn't look at me

_____

learning how to be
psychotic from the finest
coaches of psychosis—

———————

reading Hesse poems in
Sausalito (1974) and
pretending to find
beauty in them—
translated by Stephen
Spender? by Jefferson
Airplane?

———————

father is a green
mesh sieve—
mother gets poured through
sieve and the new
fluid becomes brother

———————

   what
does a powder-
blue handkerchief

in the back *right*
pocket signify?

———————

        when men
suddenly reveal
heterosexuality's
cruel trump card—

———————

mother took classes
with Robert Duncan and
Allen Ginsberg, one day
each—

———————

      my brother's
Ouija board did us
no good

———————

stomach ache
from bad snapper
sandwich after I'd made

a transatlantic phone
call saying it was a
good sandwich—

————————

an El Greco
tearful drawing

————————

goodbye, bananas, I
spent 59 cents on you
and you got squashed—
this morning you were
lovely and intact but now
you are formless and ruined—

————————

I'm
always mentioning the
Maginot Line these days,
please explain my love
affair with the Maginot
Line—

————————

          not sewn into
tapestries but left as
petite ruins for later
passersby in search
of religious stimulation—

_____

early cataract in my left
eye, Dr. Amico says—
hardening of both eyeballs,
something dangerous
on the surface—

_____

          I failed my
trumpet teacher by not
returning the Hovhaness
concerto score

_____

why do straight men
want to hang out with me?
why does the *Iliad* exist?

_____

three-
berry gay marmalade,
low-brow novels, low-cut
novels

_____

songs
on Creamsicles

_____

friend or foe
crank-called me,
one summer afternoon in
seventh grade, to ask how
many push-ups I could do

_____

cereal of choice (my mother's)
was Concentrate and so
we called her morning face
(disgruntled and depressed)
"Concentrate face"

_____

father's
professorial hairline a
bee-sting enemy fortification

———————

I enjoy
masochism, it's an
accustomed position,
and accustomed positions
are always comfortable

———————

we saw *Marnie*
with a boy just entering puberty—
he hugged the dog while
Tippi Hedren underwent
frigid conniptions, hair
designed by Alexandre de Paris—

———————

expand like
a sunflower
pissoir

———————

someone farted in the art
supply store, near the masking
tape—genderless,
like most gas

———————

a woman
with blind-seeming hooded eyes
stood in front of me on line
for the rest-stop toilet,
her boyfriend's calf muscles
under-developed

———————

a bagel in San Francisco
at David's Delicatessen
before *Company* (the touring
production)

———————

Jon Vickers sang
"Esultate" more liquidly in 1959

———————

falling in love
with a photo of someone
dead before I was born

———————

two days
after dying you're still
hooked up to the living
but by the third day the
connection fades

Trance Notebook #13

[shaving errors on Perry Street]

learning
how to use a computer
in 1988 by writing a poem
(in MS-DOS) called "Fleet
Week," homage to sexy
sailors filling West Side streets

———————

has
your college-age
daughter seen your
penis or
seen you weep?

———————

one boy on top of another boy—
I long for a repetition
hug under awning
in sudden summer rainshower

———————

tearful on phone at 7 a.m.
curly-haired daughter
of butcher announces
butcher-father's death

_____

the subject supposed to know,
the butcher-father supposed
to know—

_____

giving his son advice
on underarm odor (conquering it)
and wet dreams

_____

corpse position is the only salvation—
not wishing to be a corpse
but wanting the liberties
that come with corpse position—

_____

I apologized for the
possibly hegemonic or

ideologically fraught nature
of a subject-verb-
object sentence—

───────────

coughed five times
in pool, one cough
unbelievably satisfying—
shocking degree of
pleasure I get from
a good phlegmy hack

───────────

ask him about
Lotte Lenya and Sylvère
Lotringer, use commas
more liberally

───────────

bat mitzvah
marred by Walt Whitman
going in circles

───────────

hands Uriah-Heeping, glee
over my birthday, supposed
glee, I wax eloquent
over supposed glee

————————

Sunday night
laundry is oasis—
don't say "oasis" 300 times

————————

fear of
non-flirtation, abyss (*le
néant*) of non-flirtation

————————

no wish for sex
with anyone but intense wish
for sex-vibe experienced
randomly with everyone

————————

Virginia Johnson
(of Masters and Johnson) died

today—she helped revolutionize
the study of female orgasms,
inserting camera in vagina

—————

parrucchiere's belt pressing
against me, the tease of
his hard buckle

—————

old
ladies eating hamburgers
together as big celebration
every Thursday night—
do weekly hamburgers
reinforce ideology?

—————

hegemony is Gramsci's
concept, but did other
thinkers also invoke
hegemony?

—————

is hegemony
connected to hedgehog or
circus?

—————

dream: babysat
for a boy, precocious,
rambunctious, cultural—
his parents had no fears
about my chaperonage

—————

also two girls, one was fat,
the other (who stayed
in her room) anorexic—
punctum was seeing her
dangerously skinny arm

—————

out of dream his jeans are
tight but tight jeans in
themselves are semi-
otically ambivalent

––––––––––

critic's shame over morbidly
obese mother on escalator

––––––––––

     buying sheet
music on Mass. Ave.,
Briggs & Briggs, buying
Chopin ballades and scherzi—
Dietrich Fischer-Dieskau's
Rigoletto too expensive yet desired

––––––––––

attempt a science fair project
on whether gay men prefer
seducing straight men

––––––––––

     my father
gave my sister Ho Hos
or Ding Dongs for breakfast

––––––––––

Jewish men always
OK as subject of sentence
or object of preposition—

———————

parade of
guys looking like Peter Falk
in *Woman Under the
Influence*—

———————

starved for a Shiro plum
or a peach second—I
want ingestion and all
I get is purge and extrojection

———————

I know how to
scumble but don't know
what "scumble" means

———————

shaving errors on Perry
Street—shaving errors on
Hudson and 14th—

———

Foucault singing
anapests at the Mine
Shaft, elegaic couplets

———

—don't
keep saying "Stabat Mater"
as if it meant anything—

———

my next book is *not*
I repeat *not* about sleeping
pills—

———

don't say "parsing,"
don't use parentheses
(GRID an early name
for AIDS)

———

two
yarmulkes plus two

yarmulkes equal five
yarmulkes because Yahweh
is the fifth, secretly
walking among them—

————

    Liszt's "Forest
Murmurs" followed by
"Gnome Dance"—I vastly
preferred "Forest Murmurs"
but spent more time
practicing "Gnome Dance"—

————

jam session (jam
sestina?) with long-donged
Bob the trombone player
in seventh grade—

————

        eye
surgeon in waffle stompers
and white undershorts when
daughter vomits in
Yosemite cabin—

—————

    oft-revisited
dubious memory of
philosopher's son with
sick foot—was it
clubfoot, sprain, bruise,
or was he merely fatigued?

—————

    why is
that memory so
luminous?

—————

    it has no
apparent significance
(but appeared to me
the day before my
mother's stroke)

—————

philosopher's son
was Pip, hero
of *Great Expectations*—

————————

did the philosopher's
son have great expectations?

————————

son of a philosopher
not a bad thing to be—

————————

I'm not a philosopher
but I'm son of a philosopher—

Trance Notebook #14

[cut it up and then project it]

on Mercer Street
a burst of unnecessary
verbalization   .

————————

      ashamed of dirt
patches on white jeans

————————

      shoulder sore from
carrying black and white
gesso tubs—
figure out their weight,
dear nonexistent reader

————————

not many people know
what the inside of a
vagina during sex
looks like she said

————————

Obama and Hillary Clinton
had a top-secret
lunch today

————————

if the lunch was top-secret
why do I know about it?

————————

nothing to draw without
hair's filigree
to stabilize the gaze

————————

his face in my ass
even if I don't
want his face
in my ass even
if I'm supposedly
enjoying it—

————————

tuber-shaped penis
shoved up me though

I said no and made
my eyes go blurry
in honor of his need—

———————

supposedly gargantuan
but then it turned out
to be puny—

———————

psychotic husband
didn't pamper
the bipolar martyr who
bragged about her
Baccarat as if it were
God's little acre

———————

if your desire to write
dies a natural death,
what happens to residual
urges, the *Aeneid,*
Roger Federer, crunch
of goy eating chocolate?

————————

tall guy on subway I
disabused of false notion
that I was cruising him

————————

Mr. Baer gave me his
stamp collection but wasn't
a pervert

————————

we met at a cello concert—

————————

did I adequately
thank Mr. Baer?

————————

a fat portfolio of rare
stamps to add to my
impoverished collection

————————

how did the news travel
to Mr. Baer that I

collected stamps and wanted
supplements to my horde?

_____

why did Mr. Baer
choose me as
beneficiary of his
enigmatic gift?

_____

         tell
me more about Mr. Baer

_____

was he Jewish
or German or neither
or both?

_____

        was his primary
allegiance to stamps or
cello music?

_____

or was his
primary allegiance to
little Jewish boys
who collected stamps
and had an unsatisfied
hunger to expand their
collections?

————————

the Mr. Baers of the world
never receive adequate
emotional compensation
for their mysterious largesse—

————————

here's the secret:
cut it up and then
project it

————————

afraid
of nonreciprocation's abyss
although I am prime
among nonreciprocators

————————

if I become "deep"
will newfound depth
be the death of me?

————————

pink triangle glut—
too much "gay" in my paintings

————————

seroconversion
needn't disqualify Romeo
from entering me

————————

lava's my beldame

————————

Alessandro's basket
may become my hand's condo—
convince him to swerve

————————

write a fashion poem
tomorrow while smoking grass—
use words as bow ties

—————

syntax a baby I know
how to pamper,
syntax a baby
I know how to
miscarry—

—————

20 vigorous or semi-
vigorous minutes
next to a guy with
the droopiest balls
I've ever seen

—————

when the pen itself
takes on a mother's
putative softness

—————

too bloated to eat
grandmother cake

———————

"your book isn't AIDS-y
enough to qualify
for my blog"

———————

should I reject
figuration (still lives,
crucifixes, saints in flames,
men in jocks, pin-ups
eating each other out)?

———————

bought white miso
and made my first miso-
incorporating dish

———————

bought Creeley's edition
of selected Whitman
poems on Union Street

in the late '70s
and got stuck on the first
ode's weird word,
"eidólons"—

————

in a station wagon
parked on Union
I puzzled over "eidólons"
and rejected it
although "Eire," "dreidel,"
and "eiderdown"
lay buried
in that awkward
noun—

————

and now
I'm the kind of fool
who uses words like
"eidólon," unpopular
words with unkempt
beards—

————

I've never
once grown a beard
though yesterday
I came close

———————

      give stubble's
eidólon one more day
to blossom
into a semi-plausible
object—

Trance Notebook #15

[the opposite of Tupperware]

pallid and underage
Oscar Mayer
Wiener cocktail
hot dogs in their
stinky liquor—

_____

      cruelty inflicted
in Oscar Mayer pigpens?

_____

two-year-old boy died of
leukemia after being
best man at his
parents' wedding—

_____

I sent my mother
a subscription to the
New York Times,

large-print edition,
though I'm not sure
she can read—

———————

guy without a shirt, red
hair, pants falling down,
backpack, Woodstock-
generation nudist

———————

lay on floor for half hour,
googled "nervous breakdown
symptoms," discovered
that I *always* have
the symptoms of a
nervous breakdown—

———————

fell into a reverie about
asking the interviewer
to pose nude for me or
somehow making it
clear that he could
invite himself to strip—

————

I wonder what my
father would say about
nervous breakdowns,
the type of subject
that fuels his eloquence—

————

don't overuse
the word "rape" as
(manic)
metaphor for my own
writerly rapaciousness—

————

tomorrow draw
another crucifixion

————

sexy guy entering
café thinks I'm over-ogling
him and resembles icy-
demeanored artist
whose neck I hovered
near in pursuit of musk—

———

eviscerating envy
of sailor
hat akimbo
on crew-cut head

———

Li'l Abner "I'm
Past My Prime"—why do
I find that song so haunting?

———

because I
don't remember the singer's name?
because she *isn't* past
her prime?

———

what is a prime,
anyway?

———

and why did I already
feel past my prime when
I was seven years old?

————

    outdoor hunk
with tight green shorts
rides away
on black bike and
wasn't aware of my
existence—

————

we talked about
Lana's daughter Cheryl
Crane—"our younger listeners
probably don't know
who Lana Turner is—"

————

    learning
how to make cursive
capital T's and Z's
in elementary school—
I never made the
Z correctly—
we rarely
have recourse to a
capital cursive Z—

————

haunted by Liza with a
Z and other renounced,
betrayed Z's—

————

one symptom of a
nervous breakdown is
social avoidance, my
specialty—

————

my father maybe
relieved to leave Venezuela
in an era before
international long-distance calls
were affordable—

————

teaching me how
to urinate standing up

————

why did we call it
a pee-pee-thing?

an ordinary
suburban locution?

_____

Twinkie defense,
Listeria, hand job,
God going commando

_____

—God's
love affair with Otto Rank,
God's love affair with
Simone de Beauvoir—

_____

God's revisions of Kafka's
"Penal Colony" before
Kafka finished writing it

_____

Miss Paul was my
second-grade teacher,
Miss Paul a funny
name, like
Miss Joe or Miss
Bob or Miss Peter

———————

masturbate on the top
bunk if you're a girl,
on the bottom
if you're a boy—

———————

every time I ask
permission she
looks aggrieved—
says "are you
eating celery?"

———————

despite the taboo against
cannibalism

———————

it depends
what fish are used
in the gefilte fish—

———————

death's
interpreter, I'm

a fat man leaning on
the same banister
Kafka's uptight
virile father
leaned on

———————

if he's so famous
why do I need to ask
this question?

———————

the answer is Pink Floyd

———————

Thomas
Bernhard, *My Prizes*:
"The problem is
always to get work done
while thinking that work
will never get done
and nothing will ever
get done ..."

———————

—the *ranimer*
club—*ranimer* the
phrase Anna Moffo
sings in Debussy's
"La mort des amants"—
to reanimate

———————

profound divas
like Tupperware
or like the opposite
of Tupperware

———————

flowers like escalators

———————

"using" means
rubbing my eyes, their
chalcedony derrières

———————

Kirk Douglas's "slippage,"
my eagerness to talk
about Kirk's slippage

_____

one night we had roseate
nipples and blue mistletoe,
one night we were slapped
by our Baden-Baden painter
boyfriend at a bar

_____

like a long orgasm in
Dynagroove

_____

"Sempre libera" backwards
like Paul McCartney's death
revealed by playing
"Revolution 9" backwards—

_____

who taught
me that trick?

_____

rescued or adopted by
a queer on Mission
Street in pursuit of

his perfect éclair,
his Patricia Neal
impersonation

———————

inégale Baroque music in
Death Valley

———————

    simple indigo
riposte to mystical
cupcake-pink boxes,
Maurice's Bakery

———————

their glazed
French twists
an untimely message
never measured

Trance Notebook #16

[nights illuminated by imperishable clutter]

too late to become a
treasured scion of
a New York political
dynasty

_____

every time the line
breaks I ache

_____

I wish I could
go back in time
to give Philip Roth a blow
job when he was 21

_____

to avoid artifice

_____

the problematic
unwritten opera by

Leoš Janáček —
O souvenir, o
death of lovers—

————

       —but how can
I reach the portal of the stars
if I don't violate
some unknown god's
threshold?

————

     is there an
undead father I could
reach through Facebook?
are all fathers conceptual?
is he the culprit or
ceiling that interferes with
my "mystically blown"
inspiration?

————

blown on Varick Street
by the husband of
a noted Marxist historian

————

     his promiscuity
attracts me, his aura
of easy availability
combined with a bank
account

————

and yet it seems Rilkean
to mention this wish,
this non-wish, this
phantasmal chip

————

       mother
of thank-you notes and
elegy, Coty perfume,
the ardor of Coty
when you are
my only pleasure

————

I like your neck I
said to the grizzled
man on the bench but

in fact I don't
like his neck

_____

nights illuminated by
imperishable clutter

_____

cut on my leg I know
not from whence you came,
cut on my leg I know
not whether you are already
septic

_____

when the toilet
(in the dream) backed up,
turds found a new home
in my mother's bathroom
sink, stolen masterworks
from Boston Museum of
Fine Arts also afloat

_____

my mother didn't own
a pressure cooker

———————

my saxophonist
friend's mother owned
a pressure cooker
and praised its foolproof
efficiency—

———————

her cookies
when fresh tasted stale,
and when stale tasted fresh—
I loved their in-between position,
straddling novelty
and obsolescence—

———————

as when
a nervous traveler on
the interstate
leaves a turd (why
not?) for posterity

———

Marlowe left *Doctor
Faustus* for posterity and
Edward II

———

I taught
the poker-in-anus
scene from *Edward II*—
why doesn't the murder
occur offstage, where
tragic violence belongs?

———

imagine
Chris Burden–style
shooting myself at my
reading

———

why do I find
that a comforting thought?

———

the smell of
cheap Masonite wood
panels and the death
drive and the company
we keep

—————

or
Germaine Tailleferre, a
name I was afraid
to mispronounce—

—————

I know how to evoke
horoscopes from soiled
napkins, as in
the asylum where Liberty
prints are forbidden
and Gerald Ford is still
president

—————

I stole cocaine from
the rich son's
overcoat pocket

———————

I didn't take
the concept of criminality
seriously in those days,
I stepped into sin
as into a wading pool
on a hot summer day

———————

find the common ground
shared by Mia Farrow
and Chef Boyardee, and
don't indulge in "stop-
and-frisk" tactics with my own
cerebration—

———————

men have
boorish body language,
women have other
problems but not usually
the problem of boorish
body language

———————

      to dislike a
sound is to cast it
as the enemy and
therefore to solidify
unhappiness

———————

I admired his use
of "abeyance,"
a word like "elegiac,"
intrinsically beautiful
in its dove-like brooding
over the abyss it describes—

———————

nasal fool light blue
sublunary excitement

———————

      blood
stain on mattress, Lita
Gray, Chaplin's child
bride

———————

strawberry stains on my white
pants inevitable as a
wattle

_____

           I gave
five dollars to a
homeless painter named
Dwayne last night,
he tried to give me a
painting but I refused

_____

Anne Carson's thuggish
tone in her Euripides
translations

_____

           I seek
a thuggish tone

_____

asemic or dwelling
on the happy border

between asemic and semi-
sensible

————————

his hair feels brambly
and crinkly under a
cotton T-shirt—

————————

    what does
a ring on the middle
finger of a man's
right hand mean?

————————

to reach a point
where mania
masquerades as
regular, not unreal

————————

ceaseless murmuring
of Echo after I stole
her voice—

————

guy with
beard and white jeans
reading Benjamin's
Kafka essay on the F
train to Brooklyn—
wedding ring on left hand,
married position—
he got off at Bergen

————

a famous
Balthus painting of
Delphine Seyrig?
of Pasolini
interviewing
Carol Channing?

————

the Rhône flows with
Carol Channing's tacit
approval

————

dying to intrude into the
sovereignty of others
I am in second grade
receiving wanted or unwanted
attention for excessive fervor—

———————

under a footbridge singing
"Can't Buy Me Love"
a serendipitous
bird *incroyable*

———————

why does
"Lugano" or "Locarno"
or "Arno" recur with
the obsessiveness of Arlo
Guthrie's "Alice's Restaurant"?

———————

spinal chord *idée fixe?*

———————

theory at a standstill,
Delphine Seyrig at a standstill

———————

Trismegistus? who is the
Hermes that poets are
always talking about?
—some blowsy hermaphrodite
who slowly
attained instantaneity

Trance Notebook #17

[the lake and the kink]

every time I kiss
Thomas I grab his
face to feel the stubble

———————

dreamt I was on stage
with Liz in *Giant* or *Cat
on a Hot Tin Roof,* a
new live version, I
could tell (from her perfume)
that she was epic

———————

    dreamt I
tried to buy liquid
paper but the bottle
broke

———————

rock diva's eyes damaged
by too much plastic
surgery

———————

Hydrox cookies, sister's
cravings

———————

    did he leave
his hairy belly exposed
especially as a feast to
taunt my eye?

———————

spike has 3 meanings,
all are (St. Sebastian)
site-specific

———————

        nonstop
frequenting of tearooms in
Albany, at 16 years

old already a pedophile,
Internet whore, identity thief

_____

voices of men in
the army are
abdominal he said

_____

Commie scares
in mandarin orange
sections

_____

his balls unremarkable
for a rocket scientist
or a card shark or
a literary charlatan

_____

la chambre
est une veuve, the chamberpot

_____

        (fable
of the delicatessen's id)

_____

il marche avant la
guerre, he memorized
Costa-Gavras's *Z*

_____

il arrive sous la terre,
a wire is loose

_____

                il pleut
dans la chute, it
pulsates and churns

_____

        on peut
rester ici sans angoisse,
we can stay here
thanking the insane

_____

I did an
inadequate still life mixing
the palette's colors
to compose an
innovative gray sometimes
dominated by brown
red or green

———————

a father's spittle
landing on me though
I'm not the spittle's
intended object

———————

brother blowing his nose
without Kleenex

———————

pink tourniquet
unfolding

———————

a mnemonic
device leading me to you

————

mackerel after standing-
room *Boccanegra*

————

our baby
tortoise behaved,
our train
survived radiation

————

his father-in-law's
severe sunburn a
joke for decades

————

the burnt patch
on the waiter's arm and his
reluctance to serve me

————

attempting to paint a
strawberry container but then
it turns into an Easter egg

_____

will eating an apple be
perceived as asocial
behavior?

_____

     movement is
aphrodisiacal and non-
movement is stultifying

_____

confessing my invisibility
and waiting for them to
correct me and say "you're
not invisible"—

_____

     disgusted by
filial piety and night's likeness
to day

_____

     disgusted by the lake and
the kink

————————

by the arm and
the fossil and my
capacity to love fossils

————————

by a smile
covering his jealousy like
a condom over Zeus

————————

by trumpet teachers
and hairless chests combined
with tattoos and Thin Mints

————————

disgusted by cemeteries
and think tanks,
crenellations and tadpoles

————————

by mother's oscillation from
life to death and her semi-
permanent position on that
threshold

_____

by her rectum's
appearance in
my litanies

_____

disgusted by
my imitation of
Auden and her teeth's
participation

_____

by my
Auden imitation's
resemblance to a lesion

_____

by my
reliance on one father's
homosexuality, and that
father's suddenness

_____

by my reliance on the
homosexuality of many

fathers, and their ballads,
and their descriptions of
ballads

———————

disgusted by
goldenrod's invisibility and
by song

Trance Notebook #18

[desire demands specialization]

"Salmonella"
sounds like a bitter drag queen

_____

orange
tractor in twilight,
stichomythia, dialogue as
failure

_____

don't wet
your pants when you
get excited telling
a story

_____

of Melanie and the
Carpenters I sing—and
of hours later, and their

resemblance to hours ago,
and foretelling's resemblance
to forewent—

———————

of Triscuits and the delight
they fail to bring
I sing—

———————

     of
several rich houses in
a row, their improbability
and then their disappearance
and the mourning that
ensues—

———————

     of editorial
suggestions and micro-
abrasions, of Lasik
and softball—

———————

                    am I
aware of the royal baby?

———————

and why did I
mention Judith Butler
in Brooklyn? and why
always a reliance on
ellipsis?

———————

        she sent me
a photo of her baby
boy's rear end

———————

        I overstated
my "culture of the
pause" idea, and didn't
explain it properly

———————

        of another
stagnant tractor, this one

yellow (Indian or Naples?),
I sing—

————————

of West Point and man's
second or third disobedience—

————————

of his refusal to thank or
greet, and their Germanic
likeness—

————————

of The Monster on Grove Street
and Julius' on West 10th and
my failure to write a fashion
poem I sing

————————

the wife's mouth
qualifies as pretty, but
it disturbs me, as do
her pink ballet slippers,
and his loud
crunching on chips

————————

     a trip
to Greece to see the
oracle and give it "a
piece of our mind"

————————

     of sewing
skills and knot-tying expertise
never acquired I sing—

————————

of dents in my
Bach trumpet, of a tendency
to hoard, and the cult of impersonality—

————————

of pineapple's
resemblance to male peacock
figuration—

————————

     imagine an uncle
named Ruth, and imagine
that mistake as a
cause of fluidity

————

how can I finally seize
the day, is there a day
to be seized, have I
already seized it?

————

is it already night and
too late to seize
the day? is there a difference
between day and night?

————

I seized six o'clock, but
now it's half past eight—

————

maybe
stuttering came
from wearing a foot brace

————

what
if John Cassavetes had

made *Garden of the
Finzi-Continis* and what if
Julie Harris were
its star?

———————

     let's stand
against recollection—
in our bib overalls
remember nothing

———————

     drum up intensity
to prove
I have a body

———————

do local divinities
embrace my foul
entirety?

———————

     sponges
are never antiseptic

enough, wrists are never
limp enough, dreams
are never wet enough

———————

Stickney's
restaurant, my mother
orders tuna fish sandwich
as treat from block-
lady waitress Wanita—

———————

pink
boxes are always fancy—
fancy means
(in San José) a cake
box or a second story

———————

in a world of one-story
houses a second floor
is nirvana

———————

Mother calls to say
"I'm in a very
terrible mood,
I want to
talk to you"

_____

not wanting to seem an
East Coast snob,
I didn't mention Heidegger—

_____

nectarine or peach?
uncertain about
the difference

_____

    are nectarines
less orange or more,
or is orange not the
primary variable?

_____

husband's
dark eyebrows, "dirty" legs,
wedding ring

—————

elegy for husbands?

—————

"desire
demands specialization" I
said to three dozen men
in a southern crab bar—

—————

square heads of the idealized
and lauded

—————

man in back room saying
"after-effect" silently
to himself

—————

tell me more about Hamlet's
desire to be a woman

Trance Notebook #19

[saloon Jews hijacked the known]

metrophage, eater
of cities

_____

party of important cats
or parrots or
Loretta Young in *Private
Number* or Donna Reed
in *Scandal Sheet,*
semi-bronzed, or Cindy
Sherman in *Cinderella*

_____

I found the original
Dorothy Gale,
her last name
a temple gong

_____

     erotic note
from my amour in

Iceland touring as slam
poet and reading Langston
Hughes qua Marguerite
Yourcenar "very funny"

———————

her most radical gesture
was pouring Maxwell
House coffee in Fort
Lauderdale

———————

       Charles
Street where assistant
professors kill themselves
with coughing fits

———————

      the son's
pubic hair mentioned on
censored podcast—

———————

God like a yelping dog—

———————

forbid him to publish
his roman à clef

———————

        don't start
Kate Hepburn self-
congratulation

———————

      offer instead a complete
recital of dwindling resources

———————

      ingrown hairs
in horizontal neck crease

———————

      don't tell
your son that the first
note was wrong, he
will permanently remember
his error

———————

I'm supposed to be intimate
with my parents' corpses

_____

      haunted by female
pedophiles

_____

Barbara Stanwyck's known
lesbianism or is it
Claudette Colbert on a
Miami balcony, a memory
module?

_____

      "is Lana
a monad?" I asked the class

_____

autistic sons with prematurely
husky voices and long penises
learning how to put on
underarm deo—

_____

Creeley never made
a pass at my mother,
I never made a pass at
Creeley, I never made
a pass at Creeley's mother,
figure out the rest—

———————

dreamt
about Glenn Ligon at high
speed, his kindness, or a spasm
of being snubbed by Lotte Lenya
on a panel discussion

———————

her claim to be directly
descended from Bauhaus
gentry

———————

I was an extra in Tebaldi's
Bohème, also
in Milanov's *Trovatore,*
but in *Trovatore* everyone
on stage must sing—

———————

he holds
two-year-old boy accountable
for hyperactivity and word
prowess

———————

he dictates fairy
tale for his son gratefully to transcribe

———————

always separated from father
by office's frosted glass and
economy stairwells—

———————

how can every college
afford a philosophy department?

———————

why did my father give me
the geography department secretary's
phone number?

———————

tyrannized by consecutiveness

_____

Germanic upside-down mouth
and Genghis Khan
pianism (cocktail eyeglasses)

_____

sleep the sleep of the
braceleted, her kink
lipstick off-white

_____

      tardive
dyskinesia intrudes on
cinematic réclame

_____

      I own an
8mm copy of the complete
Intolerance

_____

      literature
will always be a good

vehicle for discussing
death—I can warm
up for the real deaths by
saying "my stepfather
died" because stepfather
was just a word

_____

finding
salvation in the curve of
my L.L.Bean bag

_____

describe the dismembered
cardboard boxes I painted on

_____

she's
always in the midst of
a bowel movement and
always narrating it

_____

when no teeth
are left in her
mouth, when
I take on the no teeth

—————

poet on subway gave
same spiel in two cars

—————

woman in wheelchair
with prosthetic leg
displayed hook
and then ate pistachios

—————

extra cum dripped down
my leg, translucency
like soft gloss acrylic gel

—————

saloon Jews hijacked
the known

—————

diseased
political theorist with leg
scabs on West 44th near
demolition

———————

sweeping the yard,
taking too seriously
her command to remove leaves
from red rocks, taking too seriously
petty exhibitions I undergo
as servitude—

———————

words from
William James today are
raisin, egg, pinch, bit,
field

———————

first line of "Sunday
Morning" pronounced
with Russian accent

———————

becoming the incorrigible
father's forearm underside

_____

thick naked thighs in
galley kitchen behind
distorting glass

_____

a "nancy"
man, topless, with hog pants

_____

her nurse-mother's
chalk or butterscotch hair

_____

my heart
is breaking she said when
brother sold the house

_____

mother alone
in bed with brother

―――――――

again and again speaking to
the baby, trying to figure
out how to make it happy

―――――――

the doctor said
"she is bent
but not broken"

―――――――

a dubitable
diagnosis I'm not
supposed to report
lest its subject shatter
into half-tone dots

Trance Notebook #20

[self-slaughter and poppies]

"fascistic" not a
word to use lightly

_____

failing to pay my son's
tuition and lying about
the failure

_____

all narrators are
unreliable, all narrators are
fathers, even if they are
daughters they are also
secretly fathers—

_____

a purple nose worthy of
Holbein or Hals

_____

I want the freedom to
use the word "nosology"

———————

wanting
desperately to lean into his
body because of its girth

———————

deciding to drop
my family has caused
parallel derelictions

———————

bangs of she who idolized
me in a borrowed apartment

———————

onions are
affordable, bisexuals are
not affordable

———————

tendency
to incarnate a sticky
cupcake—

_____

fewer impediments make for
saintly existence—

_____

a mind returning
to taboo haunts, spandex
at overnight camp,
marshmallows grilled
on graham crackers as
new raison d'être

_____

she didn't know the haunted
house poem and yet
he kept pestering her,
meanwhile pretending to be
her staunchest advocate—

_____

it travels through the circle
of fifths that I am
a snob recluse

———————

     Lindbergh's kidnapped
son, wrinkled fold near
namby-pamby pink ear

———————

playing doctor not for love
of underwear but for love
of driving to restaurants—

———————

funny hamster face of man
who advocates
poison gas—

———————

Henry James's
Fleda Vetch—
Leda or flee?

———————

suddenly visualizing
three-tiered vagina on Sealy
Posturepedic mattress

─────────

          he was
her husband, I
was her bursar

─────────

    plenty of salt
on cold spaghetti—is that
a film, *Plenty of Salt*,
porno necessity?

─────────

    8-track
tape enthroning
Barbarella friction—

─────────

bright light but no subject
matter, just offal and
ducks and Frank Zappa fans

————————

watching *The Exorcist* on
my smartphone to pass
the time—how many
hours till Linda Blair's
head speaks to my people?

————————

The Lady
Vanishes after she munches
on chicken wings

————————

Dad in
drenched dirndl
at the World
Economic Forum, Davos,
spinning a dreidl

————————

dapper yes-man's
seminar on Hinduism
or Cruise Ship
Etiquette

————————

     cute guys
ride in a separate
padlocked caboose

————————

     he smells
of lightly toasted caca,
similar to pine nuts or
burnt cornmeal—

————————

János Starker's nicotine
addiction helped his Bach

————————

a Brandy Alexander approach
to getting the most out of
your first visit to the
Guggenheim

————————

     compilation
of other gestures, performed

wildly and repetitively and
with infantile
presumption—

————————

      any God will do,
I'll take Hephaestus—
a necromancer but also
the Jewish mystical expressway
Gloria Swanson needs—

————————

      oral sex a
Walser specialty

————————

      Graham Bell's mouth
a slub-fest

————————

      Leigh
Hunt stayed in my
room 150 years ago—
Leigh Hunt had a
speech impediment

————

    I wanted to say
"kettle chips" hours ago and
didn't allow myself

————

      curly-
haired (or marcelled)
guys with amphetamine
hubris

————

    all her
teeth are falling out, she
keeps them in a change purse

————

     porcelain withered
creased skin of my
ancient Tante Alice
who was only 75—
I misjudged ancientness—

————

grass-
stained buttocks, repose
as goat cheese

_____

Andrews
Sisters singing "When Lilacs
Last in the Dooryard"

_____

which several rooms of
premarital existence did
Keats describe in that
famous letter to his guidance
counselor?

_____

reincarnated
milqueteoast, my
dead stepfather momently
returned to life in
the jolly corridor

_____

right now my
dead stepfather
planning entrance into
a new body—

_____

bad karma
of a disappeared daughter
and four stepchildren
who didn't pay him much heed—

_____

goatee and poesy—
sleep and goatee—
self-slaughter and poppies—

_____

how to
draw a layer cake,
a vanity project—

_____

the knuckle-cracker's
love of Charles Kingsley's
water-babies—

_____

        newborn
porpoises as emblem of
overeagerness to be a
good student—*Richard
III* as compulsory lifeblood

_____

        death-denying
handsome porter drunk
on his midnight stool

_____

a monstrous craving
for shrimp gumbo,
committing oneself to
shrimp gumbo, stintless
loyalty to shrimp gumbo—

_____

pimple arm next to cancer
bracelet—

_____

the new cleft-chinned
Bobby Sherman-esque
candidate for my
masochistic inner flights—

———————

Hélène Cixous gave Avital
Ronell a dozen roses
and then Avital
gave those roses to me

Trance Notebook #21

[surreptitious nookie with a large astronaut]

he held this pen and
therefore polluted it

_____

rubbing his finger
gay along lip as at
Castro Theater seeing
Giant

_____

two
penises together in photo
lead to penises together
in Winnipeg, syllogism—

_____

starting from
Paumanok is fine but where
is Paumanok and why is
it fish-shaped?

———

lining up the
anti-Semites

———

breast of
shrink in dark near
Thai Orchid—mind
and lit obelisk or observatory
scene in *Rebel without a Cause*

———

smell of AIDS in Ramrod
the young poet said

———

hurts
wrist to shake hands with
a pervert

———

is Whitman pro-onanism
or anti-onanism? obviously
both, Whitman is
pro-bowel

———————

writing in a Greyhound bus
station in a tiny pad, doing
character sketches as warm-up
for fiction

———————

   I took disco
dancing lessons near theater where
Airport played, Baskin-
Robbins afterward, kiss
or not kiss at the door

———————

  Warren Beatty's big
cock as seen by sister Shirley
MacLaine

———————

  stern
urinating at airport,
a pilot shaking it out

———————

beard of cousin proclaiming
Horowitz's "Arabeske" (Schumann)
ambrosial

———————

father's "inner" precludes my
use of "inner," father and son
can't both use "inner"—

———————

　　Wagner and Whitman
in cahoots vis-à-vis crowd
consciousness, Frankfurt School

———————

　　　　　use
book covers as canvases for
structured figure/ground
experiments

———————

copycat suicides rampant
in Europe, Werther's
Muttersprache

———————

cough cough in Munich is
racist code, they cough when
they sense difference, they
cough when they need to expel
the other, they cough when
they are uncomfortable—

———————

God stood on the mount
and said please remove
Safeway supermarket
from your memory

———————

       nightmarish
sex in cars, quick
gropes on BART

———————

underarm hair is turbulence

———————

Idiot
epilepsy mentioned in conjunction
with élève and Spontaneous Me

———————

gunshot wound
mentioned in jest

———————

rush is *Rausch,*
Rausch isn't quite trance

———————

ressentiment said
the admirer of Nietzsche
despite crazy son, crazy wife,
bad aortas

———————

red Converse
sneakers as signature of
early nostalgia

———————

Unica Zürn found
sexual stimulation in a void

————

she told me never again to
mention vagina though she
acknowledged that by over-
mentioning vagina I was
attempting to be
a vagina projectionist

————

pancakes as incest and trips to
SF to buy school dresses
for the weeper—

————

Botticelli essay researched
in Jesuit library

————

I lean on the
sentence as if it were

a stranger's leg or arm,
I lean upon the object of
the verb as if screwing it

———————

reading *Bleak House* and
Pure and the Impure on
cross-country flights, lying
to the Bible teacher

———————

anger at my son,
my non-son, my objectification

———————

strange insistence on
making surreptitious nookie
with a large astronaut

———————

fomerly epiphanic relation to
the vomiting episode

———————

she
threw herself out a window
not because Hans Bellmer
tied her up or maybe yes
because Bellmer tied her up

———————

father's
messy handwriting, legal pads
in conservatory library

———————

mortadella
or turkey for 99 cents, a
roll for 25 cents, no mustard,
no lettuce, no tomato

———————

stretched Ginsberg mouth
of poet son, imbecile nose
of automatic writer

———————

make it clear to Cher
that I consider her
a trashy runner-up
with a trashy grandmother

_____

      will the
red sneakers be thrown away?
do the red sneakers require
forgiveness?

_____

my mother made bastard
chicken for supper

_____

      stop saying "you're
sexy" to guys who won't reciprocate—

_____

stop chasing epiphenomenal
forefathers, Dutch Jews
in 1612

_____

"—ate" words
refer to extrojection
(*expectorate, regurgitate*)

_____

"—ize" words
refer to introjection
(*moisturize, internalize*)

_____

this porn photo
of skinhead is up your
alley because of menorah
frame

_____

much
I say is fantasy but
imprisoned filmmaker
is fact

_____

English poetry has spent
1,000 years counting

to ten, then
starting all over again,
iambic pentameter
a meditation hook

———————

tomato stain on hustler's
T-shirt

———————

father taught me about suicide
and recommended Dostoevsky
in the Rambler station wagon

———————

Mr. Beebee taught mother to
drive the Rambler
slowly to Santa Cruz

———————

father's secretary pretended
to be moved by Tillie Olsen

———————

Stonehenge transported by
Museum of Tolerance
to Ottawa

——————

     save our
ability to say "cloud,"
save our glances and cuckoldings

——————

give us strength to endure
the nonhorizontal

——————

     be ocean not cloud, be
land imminent

——————

no surface to call
dominant, no horizontal
plank to reign

——————

L'Immoraliste
as gift, *Steppenwolf* as intro
to drug consciousness and literary
refinement and pubic
hair triangles

————————

stability
achieved though we are
momentarily sideways

————————

broken lip on Fourth of
July threshold

————————

mother's awareness of son's
sperm, Shabbat pride

————————

Schiele's refined perverts
help us survive

————————

Smucker's jam,
rye toast, yellow eggs with
white irregular saltless lumps

Trance Notebook #22

[ultramarine has a pocky charisma]

in the past, philosopher
queen, we
majestically proposed ideas

—————

our small ugly face shoved
into back-assed Lucite chasm

—————

now I want French
scholar's maroon
velvet suit and hair

—————

                    he has
cologne I envy, money
and totality

—————

ask where he got his perfect
hair and righteousness

————————

need to figure out
every avant-garde
face in the auditorium

————————

imaginary rubs based
on accidental contiguity

————————

could he be subtly
conquered under hotel sheets?

————————

hair like a 1970s
After Dark model—

————————

can I say "I love your
look" or go door by door trying
to find a candy store?

————————

microscript a sign
of authorial integrity—

_____

years ago I was
haunted by a guy named
Didier—that was the era
of a thousand Didiers—
even at the dry cleaners
I bumped into Didier—
Jet Cleaners of Didier
fame—

_____

his hair
in French is obviously
superego-driven

_____

let him seduce me
as an indirect way
to inflict sadism on *him*

_____

Hegel
uncompromising in
support for masturbators,
Rousseau the world's
most famous masturbator—
nor forget Algernon Swinburne,
Sapphist extraordinaire

————

his name is
Ron, but Ron what?
Ron of hair and velvet
blouse and handsome
Sontag-loving boyfriend

————

making out in church
sanctuary, lights out,
herpes

————

leg hair crawls up
to bathing suit
sighted in Ludlam play

————

        kiss antique dealer
Adam's apple logorrhea in
rainstorm

————

        hard-on
at dawn merely from awareness
of self, not from other's body

————

Mitropoulos last fuck in sauna
idly available, no taker,
not friendly enough

————

        snowfall
of poet's son, envy of
poet's son in bed
with Donatello,
hair of free love

————

      thanks for your beauty,
your communism, your
Brando prostitute
demeanor

————————

      his
guitar, his gait and
orthodoxy with striped
baby, teal mom

————————

      deep
need for Pampers in
couture w/out specifics

————————

invasive sublimity
nixed, plainspoken
sublimity chosen instead—
I represent and I
don't represent

————————

I lied all morning—
Burberry tartan cutie
shoved codes onto me

———————

"nim"
is junior-high compromise
between "numb" and "him,"
or "numb" and "nimble," or
"numb" and "dim"

———————

faun worried
about hygiene, AIDS he
means not hygiene

———————

Marimekko dresses
matching shoes on bed,
light showing through
curtain reveals no under-
wear beneath caftan beard

———————

lifting me to lisp étoile

_____

how can I be lifted
by ecstasy without
betraying mother?

_____

messa di voce is impossible
diminuendo—years of
caring about perfect
diminuendi might be over

_____

sons as sticks to be
proud of, even from
afar

_____

      she abandoned
me while playing harp

_____

we sing because we hold
ourselves secret

resources apart
from imagined drunken
victories

————————

      suddenly
sentimental we
nominate those
moments as our mortal
mothers, self-slain

————————

the "qu" sound kills
interlopers who willingly
deafen themselves to avoid
immolation and melancholy

————————

      pause, gosling

————————

parallel yellow and
blue create muddy
remembered punctual green

————————

endangering the hard
explanatory brain

———————

touch his beard
again and again, greedy
suture

———————

I folded him
in half to discover
the uterine

———————

forget about imagism,
forget about "Get
Happy," forget about
narco-premiums

———————

nostril
hair entrance to coital
dorm vista, and the

pig nose attitude toward
Jewish crossdressing, Bruch,
her pixie truism—

_____

    they think
all I wear are
tank tops and wanky moons,
a winter uniform

_____

    all "o"
sounds exiled from this
stanza

_____

    or the tawdry
as a concept, his séance
and my trance

_____

    our father in
motherland

_____

Aleister Crowley anyone?
he sees the magick
difference

————————

pinks and oranges stood
out yesterday

————————

Greek extortionist with
facial damage blackmails
us in our hotel

————————

     dropping
mother off at our apartment
so she can make a series of
angry libidinal phone calls
recruiting bake sale victims

————————

she gurgles *mene*
tekel in Daniel with
shut blind eyes

———————

    "ge" appears
everywhere in German,
object attached to
verb and incidentally
migrant, like a phone
app

———————

    parked
on 23rd in the pissed-on
dark, plastic belongings
tucked into green mailbox

———————

he went to have pee and
lunch and shoot-up

———————

    prepositional
phrase's arrival at noun
in French has more tonal
variety than in English

———————

pop-up queer offerings
like Renaissance fairs
and cinammon buns

———————

I never inspected
cinammon boy's
nude thighs, their high
shut stipulated area,
closed to Cassavetes
ambiguities in 1927

———————

      man
in wheelchair sets muffin
on yellow bar stool

———————

the less hair I have
the more the dye
burns the scalp

———————

are you cut? I
want to know if you're

eligible for our dating
service, only cut men
are eligible

———————

        put
the bucket out and collect
some of the falling
rain, or is it a non-
liquid substance
falling?

———————

      the first time
I discovered Alice
was coincidentally
in an archive

———————

between the jism and the
———————, he said
blankly, derivatively

———————

                    glossolalia I
said, unsure of glossolalia's
exact significance

————————

ten thousand years ago
Raquel Welch
we were in the same tribe
on adjacent continents—

————————

I look Egyptian and Israeli
but am neither

————————

three bunnies and one
bird on yellow rectangle
concealed with
green make toxic
lawny combination—

————————

                    ultramarine has
a pocky charisma—the

noncontinuous is often
the most guileless

_____

pocky usually
modifies corpse

_____

no
comment from mother to
say she received or did
not receive the frock

_____

make drawings
without central compositional
focus

_____

fishnet stockings
on a 28-year-old Danish
married man made me
cum five times

_____

Winterreise
for ambassadors and tubas

————

    I already
said cluster fuck but where
and when did I say
cluster fuck and was it
a clear or successful use of
cluster fuck?

————

        carelessness
caused me to spill
water on this book
which is therefore
ruined, yet darkness
qualifies this book
as *not* ruined—

Trance Notebook #23

[alabaster concussive effect of stillbirth]

learning to value
cupcakes in a deli
window because a tree
grows outside it

―――――――

the city a
string of rejected
pearls, one rejectee per block

―――――――

learning to appreciate
each tattoo parlor's dignity

―――――――

mother flipflops
to signal instant recall of
tainted vegetables,
her paradoxical readiness
to eat ruined greens

———————

the time a student said
taint and read taint into
my Xmas gestures

———————

to enter my
classroom you must pass thru
Rick Moody's classroom, to
enter Rick Moody's classroom
you must pass thru J. D.
Salinger's classroom

———————

sigh, get out
of my chair, sad chair,
really sad chair, sad
dead lovers liking *ranimer*
in Baudelaire because *ranimer*
like a husband is pre-jizz,
instant before jizz on Sunday

———————

pink pearl, small pink
sing-along Mitch Miller
Burl Ives

————————

    Danny Thomas
said verboten, *Make Way
for Verboten, Whiskers for
Verboten,* a minor catch-all epic

————————

caring for a goat,
mourning a goat, seeking
in-laws among goat farmers

————————

the return to head cheese
as major conversational
anchor, *mémoire involontaire*'s
head cheese—stop
that all-encompassing
notion of head cheese as
the center of *mémoire
involontaire*

————

    triangulations and
climbing a ladder while
stoned, two tall guys
knowing I can't climb a
ladder while stoned, why a
ladder, why a plaid shirt,
why the rule against
repeating the plaid shirt?

————

black-figured vases
as jealousy's origin

————

jealousy has no origin

————

    cousins
are the origin of envy

————

    political conversations
at lunch are the origins

of cousin envy and cousin
eroticism

_____

Languedoc as origin
of big balls

_____

        her three-month
affair with a crossdresser
who no longer considers
intention (intentionality?)
a crossroads

_____

to be thrown into existence
versus thrown like a plate
of spaghetti on the piano
teacher's motherly wall

_____

yellow and red
and their capacity to stun
or inundate

_____

refusal to avoid
fuchsia

_____

quinacridone
magenta is the magic key
to reversing the subject/
object binary

_____

quinacridone
magenta has the power
to see me, and therefore
quinacridone magenta,
as Benjamin said, has
aura

_____

aura, an
object's ability to gaze
at a viewer, an object's
volition, superior
to a groveling human's

_____

      our regret
that we are not a
novelist, we are too
lazy to be a novelist, our
standards are at once
too lax and too stringent

_____

      —stalled at
sunset on a river
bank like H.D. imagining
herself as Prosperina
or Eurydice, the ones
left behind, pampered
and then rejected

_____

developing strategies of not
moving, hour after hour
of heedless inscription

_____

no
knowledge of how to perform
sumi-e techniques

———————

the man who cut off
his own ears in prison
was handsome, even
without ears

———————

nerves nerves nerves like
Jerusalem or rabies—

———————

demonizing my newest
love isn't the solution,
writing on a paper bag by
moonlight might be the solution

———————

make a decision
about how to frame
continuousness

—————

    —hoodie
on prematurely aged hunk
with a fit of shyness,
non-response despite my
death confession (perhaps
my tone toward death
was offputtingly flippant?)

—————

Delilah has ringlets but
no one wants to cut them off—
everyone considers
Samson hot

—————

        I misdefined
libido and passively
snubbed the Corsican savant
because he wouldn't give me
a blow job

—————

anatomically
a giant cock goes well
with your "visionary capacity"
I said in an email—
her nose and teeth
like Celan's, from
a jaundiced distance

———————

do I therefore retract
my art?

———————

does one art refuse
another?

———————

all midnights are
fifteen minutes away from
each other, a string of
midnights near enough
to kiss

———————

his facial muscles half
paralyzed from anal
surgery (elective) but
still a sexpot, desired
in empty lots

———————

a deep
listener with Honey
West mole
wants to seduce the tall
sculptor tonight though
tonight it's *my* turn to
seduce the tall sculptor

———————

in twenty minutes
folks your childhood will
be repeated

———————

widow's
projectile faux pas in

pregnancy's wine-dark
vicinity—

————————

    ask
father where in Caracas
he lived—to what
purpose?

————————

too late to pick up
a key ordered five years
ago and never claimed—

————————

    coldly evaluated
containers versus
warmly husbanded
containers, cruel
drafts in the free museum

————————

    ultramarine
hollow inside the hospital

————

hollow inside the
transition

————

action painting's disregard
for facts

————

he pronounced *tomb* like *Tom*—
tombstone becomes
Tom Stone

————

write on
irregularly shaped paper
and let fluctuations of
paper texture determine
the subject—

————

"Me and Mrs. Jones"
sung by Janis Joplin
without pausing

————

       alphabet
soup for runaway boy
when he returns—why
did he run away
from home?

————

       lingering
near red pebbles outside
the house, waiting for
mother to recognize me,
received back home by
father not mother

————

breasts of moonlighting
violist and their earlier
importance to me

————

my father coming
downstairs at midnight
to eat canned peas—

leaning his head
back to drink
pea liquor

———————

her *King Lear* paper un-
written and I'm supposed
to help her write it

———————

                    we
ostracize her because she
says I walk like a fag
but I *am* a fag so
we shouldn't have
ostracized her for
saying I walk like a fag

———————

Breton's pregnancy project—
my old fantasy of the
perineum skateboard, a
royal "we," a grand
schematic Nehru collar—

———————

    alabaster
concussive effect of stillbirth

———————

blue laid on like egg,
unheard blue
already imperial,
a repeated pattern
we grow to regret

———————

another pink layer
to cover the perishable
first coat of pink

Trance Notebook #24

[naked sailor confronting his Laocoön identity]

hydro-
consciousness—

_____

irregularity
of writing surface will
make classification
of this fragment
an impossibility,
perhaps the fragment
is posthumous
or fatherly

_____

can we include
red raincoats in
hydro-consciousness?

_____

my infancy's
duplex neighbor Marge
dead but in Hades
or paradise not
findable

———————

frayed
slicker, gums bleeding

———————

threw
myself at divinity
student, wanting to
know if I'm his
bleeding shipwrecked
sailor—

———————

again
the naked sailor
confronting his
Laocoön identity—

———————

I keep looking up
"Laocoön," and the "coön"
part never makes sense
but is intrinsic
to the legend's clout

———————

I won't
find in his body
an echo of the dead-
to-me trumpeter—

———————

Mrs. Auchincloss
took the besmirched
pink dress and hid it
in Georgetown attic
where it remains for
200 more years

———————

why not
capitalize He?
easy to become

God simply by
saying He was
flabbergasted to
fold his text in
half and thereby
puncture it—

_____

she calls twice in a row
to lay down her career
in the mud and declare
unbudgeable gloom

_____

his bow-tie nervousness
and overhistrionic charisma,
white chest hair like
collegiate Rapunzel

_____

deliberate swerves are
overcalculated islands

_____

his articulated wish
to tongue my spine

_____

piss on him
in a bathtub to repair
Axis Powers errors?

_____

the worst smell supposedly
authorized by D. H. Lawrence

_____

some stinky people have
friends despite the stink

_____

maybe the friends are
stinky too or wear masks

_____

I pretend to be in love
with stink and build
a mythology around it

_____

        stink
arises at charged moments
and then like a landmark
hotel disappears or fades
into genteel negligibility

—————

perhaps good readers
stink, their devotion
to fiction a foul odor

—————

        plot
stinks, policiers
stink, transvestism
undercurrents stink

—————

we won't try to spin
the stink or rotate it
backward—

—————

        I say
"yeah" too many times,

unconsciously, and perhaps
my "yeah" stinks

_____

    stink returns
like gentrification, a
sump or sere stink known to
fathers who smell it and
mothers who boycott it

_____

    long ago
this refrain was whispered
into my ear on Long
Island, where I was
confidant of the stink's
mother

_____

    note stink's
pornotopic features, its
reluctance to commit, its
non-enthusiasm and minima
moralia

_____

I start to get ambitious
in the presence of stink

———————

we dwelt
in marble halls of stink

———————

perhaps the
stink memorizes Sara
Teasdale or am I
Sara Teasdale fearing
stink—art's enemy?

———————

stink without concision

———————

The Oscar stink,
Sweet Bird of Youth
stink

———————

united by affection for
stink art

———————

       we
depart from stink and
arrive at
Stink Termini

———————

Stink Aleph,
expectorated molecule of
ecstasy as written
three times on God's nipple

———————

God like most men
and women has two
nipples and one is the
stinky nipple—

———————

      even in
pitch black night
the stink has
lumen to guide it—

Trance Notebook #25

[choose grope partners among the
Eddie Fishers and Tony Curtises]

in my presence he called
himself surrealist horndog and I
took the designation seriously

————————

skin accustomed
to puncture cannot
court puncture
or willingly assume
posture of *poignardé*

————————

fuga is name of man's cleft,
his vestigial vagina

————————

grandiosity and
talking faster than usual
are signs of mania

———————

his ass opened for my
inspection is a direct
quote

———————

    I trash this book
like Prospero
accused of forgery

———————

    dim eyes of
musical comedy love—
why didn't I mention
Barbara Cook, Dee Dee
Bridgewater, ethical
nearness of man in the
glass box?

———————

    no one talks
anymore about Dr. Reuben's
Ben-Wa Balls

———————

skeptical straight
boys bonding
over fluorescent
orange and taxis, farts
in BarcaLoungers,
novelistic opprobrium

_____

change right dolmen
to manganese blue so
it doesn't look like
a man

_____

grazed his butt with
my bow tie as he passed
through orchestra

_____

lust
on Internet more real
than lust in reality

_____

dreamt
of breasts? startling
and out of circulation

———————

Rex
Harrison's son died

———————

gone the quick grope
crowd—scheduled manic
buttocks asymmetrical

———————

loosened schizoid
liberatory art teacher

———————

right-wing sage's anus mouth
in Ginsberg TV interview

———————

they piece me together
from anciens régimes

_____

two hydrangeas
typify castration
to whom?

_____

    I am the pebble
or pavingstone he stepped on
to reach his Wikipedia entry

_____

    becoming a person
who doesn't remember names,
becoming an instrument
of penal colony torture

_____

not pausing because
pausing is Nellie Forbush
picnic pathos

_____

strategies for Thom
Gunn's basket to
be reincarnated

————————

grandfather took
granddaughter to the men's
locker room today
and I hid my Noah nude
massiveness so grand-
daughter wouldn't get excited

————————

Noah showed dead sea
testicles to stunned
stunted progeny

————————

love Lucio
Fontana's punctured
canvases?

————————

Mayflower heir
brings paintings
of nude Christ and Magdalene
to deli and accidentally
leaves them near salad

bar's hardboiled eggs
and chicken wings

————————

in Plateau 7 restaurant
elevator my grandfather
asks, "How many people
in this elevator are
Jewish?"

————————

she doesn't understand abstract
art so how can I
trust her verdicts on my
psychotic ideation?

————————

who in Darwin's *Origin*
masquerades as Ingres?
as Delacroix?

————————

is Delacroix's mother palsied?
a climax? a Tcherepnin

small piece like gavotte
or gigue for handclappers?

_____

with all my pathetic
young heart I want to
audition for Junior
Music Festival

_____

playing whatever
measly repertoire I can
command

_____

favorite kid
in the universe dressed
as ghost for Halloween
and held a bright orange
carrot as scimitar
in his oral hand

_____

preemptive
Kaddish for the not dead

mother she did not love—
or did she treat her mother
better than I treat mine?

————————

choose grope partners
among the Eddie Fishers
and Tony Curtises

————————

13th Street
back in time to Violetta's
Mexican restaurant Saturday
night euphoria with rice
for $7.99 and free
demitasse coda—

————————

librarian
dissing me, claiming
ChapStick on Highway 101,
Italo-Teutonic philosopher's
scent at whirlpool
not manifest

————————

    and my failure to
measure up to showering
triangular crotch
hair sighted in Yosemite
bathroom mirror—
a failure tantamount
to *Rosenkavalier* trio
climax without peer

Trance Notebook #26

[jade plant phallus lopped off]

rouged son and mother
finagling a luxe
hotel room in monsoon
Tokyo

––––––––––

my belly, what
kind of belly?

––––––––––

doomed
to be this dead body
that discovered the cure
for Lyme disease

––––––––––

jade plant phallus
lopped off and now recovering
in plastic cup

––––––––––

jade plant
phallus removed will
thrive in Ajax test tube

———————

Formica
test tube baby loves its
non-love environment, a
Huggie doctrine like
Nefertiti's or Monroe's

———————

bloody cut on right thumb
from ill-handled corkscrew

———————

not one nice comment
about my body though I told
him I'm "phallically
organized"

———————

orthodox Jew named Eddie
with semi-hard-on watching,
happy to watch

———

uneventful ass

———

she calls mine
"a graphic investigation"

———

much to say about
color blocks
the stranger indicated

———

blow job
avoids avalanche
of phone messages

———

Eddie repeatedly
itching his groin

———

v-patch at neck of
waiter needs close

discussion and dissection—
occasion for graphic
investigation?

_____

      a war of
wills, trying to get
stud to say hello to me

_____

      poppy seed
filling and engorged pearl
barley soaked in sour
cream and kirsch, then
fava beans

_____

peacenik sweatshirt and
"dialectical" smirk

_____

      we prefer Richard III to
Lady Day, but one of us,
the mother, prefers Lady

Day, and it grows more
vertical

_____

to investigate lacerations
the married muralist
needs a cubbyhole

_____

Miró as lost underground
treasure, dropsical

_____

          now
this conversation must end

_____

   tranquil trees
between 26th and
29th Streets, I cross avenue
when arbor ends

_____

one man
at dark back of DVD
Explosion mart

—————

or Marsden Hartley whose
archaic nude I resemble

—————

oil-stained
driveway where suicidal
neighbor butt crack waits,
slowly repairing car

—————

"affective"
mentioned in same
breath as Dennis Cooper's
The Sluts

—————

chlorine smell, his smooth
movement into another nude
guy's conversational space

———————

yet perhaps I've not made
the transition elegantly

———————

suddenly
a perfect excuse
to receive a blow job without
scrutinizing whether the donor
is worthy of giving it

———————

trans
boy or girl who
wears Mary Janes

———————

or the tender
shoot and shush of a
father

———————

and the spanked
ass of a son's sent
email

———————

he laughs at "poesis"
or was the phrase
"spinach poesis"?

———————

on black panel, yellow
Flashe paint offers
spotty coverage

———————

        rosyfingered
boy pretending he's Diane
di Prima or Sontag on
Riverside Drive circa
I, Etcetera or Shulamith
Firestone

———————

        fifth-grade
Hebrew school class and torn
fishnet stockings as grape
aggressiveness

———————

acrostic blazon's
teardrop commas
screwing me

———————

hissing hissing and her
President-Reagan-loyalty
(Silence = Death?)
to Keith Haring's mother-
meds

———————

always
omphalos in Keith,
always ouroborosly in Keith,
as in Gertrude Stein's
Lynn or Lyon

———————

Rowan
and Martin's *Laugh-In*
and Richard Pryor subject
to abjecting laughter

———————

sparrow's or starling's
or pheasant's self-conscious
atopicality

————————

I don't have an easy
or unembarrassing way
of remedying it

Trance Notebook #27

[nostalgia for the wooden nipple era]

saw landsman with micropenis
a second time and waved

—————

    a father's
genital muteness and
Ukranian upbringing
near Lvov but
not yet Lvov

—————

coma as the best year
of her life

—————

    four eyes mentioned
as slur, also faggot,
nerd

—————

shut-in mentioned as
ancient tribute

_____

which spasms in
the back are deadly?

_____

is he noticing
(amid father-wrack)
the deadly spasm or
is he a Vallée
d'Obermann episode?

_____

always mise-en-abyme
of pedophilia even if
we're not pedophiles

_____

laughing at Grey Poupon
in atrium—why is Grey
Poupon grey?

_____

was lemon
painting purchased
on that voyage?

———————

is closure a desired
result of childbirth-
style dilation
of thought's cervix?

———————

pectorals "big as vagina"
said Allen Ginsberg—
why big?

———————

I over-
praised the bridge
of his nose

———————

what does
a pacifier taste like?

———————

rabbi's infirm knowledge
of plastic nipple

_____

long-ago
poem about wooden nipple—
nostalgia for the wooden
nipple era

_____

apology for
transforming lobotomy
into three-act play—

_____

a definite stubble fiend,
Klaus Kinski's child mouth

_____

Mrs. Portnoy v. Naomi
Ginsberg intestate

_____

"ginger" he called me,
credulous of dye—

_____

              take
Book of Joshua
porn more seriously
as moneymaking venture
in Madison Square Park

_____

can straight men
always be bent?

_____

        a man at home
with his penis or not
at home with it

_____

unlocking the story
of a man at home
with his penis is not simple

_____

        kicked out for staying
three hours over a bowl of
sour cream

————————

    honk
if you're voting for
Philomela

————————

is that derogatory toward
a child star?

————————

threadbare semi-erect
teen in Van Ness
or Polk Holiday Inn,
marching band S/M

————————

flecked ivory wrist until
now unnoticed

————————

observe his
wrist and ask to pet it

————————

make his wrist my keepsake—
his crewcut my companion

———————

email him the missing
crucial syllable, like "em"
in "Eminem," or "ho" in
"homonym," or "mole"
in "molecule"—

———————

     Norma
Jeane's Christian Science birth
ein lyrisches hoax?

———————

the long typing marathon
in *They Shoot Horses,*
Don't They?, *Butch Cassidy*
drive-in anxiety attack re-
scheduled and trivialized

———————

maybe SAT chocolate,
maybe fruity skin problems,
maybe not wanting friendship
during SAT exam break

_____

"piano legs" said
the tipsy sci-fi
odoriferous penthouse
hermeneut
about himself allegedly

_____

tall view of ankles
from floor vantage,
stained taint angle

_____

Lady Be Good
Goldberg Variations
kindness to son
who wants paper clips
more than he wants

irrational shuffle-step
godhead

———————

Tricia Nixon always
appears as acoylte on
phone for adulterer's sake—
etched and bleached
Tricia, traumatized
Tricia's noblesse oblige
to Caroline

———————

wrinkle on
rotund stockbroker khaki

———————

why does that *Singspiel*
monster gape
at me and must I consider
his facial expressions sexy?

———————

three
dents were loved, all were

mentioned, I thrived on
mentioning dents, I kept
on being a non-stop dent-
mentioner—

————

      I couldn't
retire my dent mania,
I couldn't define dent,
I kept scratching the
signifier, even if it was
a dent—

————

      with emery
board I filed down
the dent to a nubbin—

————

I paused after the dent
resolved its nothingness
dilemma—

————

but I kept scratching
my gambling certificate,
an odd pock like Dentyne
pucker in plastic packet

Trance Notebook #28

[agape gape grape]

gaping
at the monster who earlier
gaped at me

_____

agape versus
gape versus grape, all
glorious by resemblance

_____

agape gape grape, their
grave importance,
the "gape" a yawning
curiosity or space where
we can gaze in search
of tonic and resolution

_____

liquor poured into the
tall water jug, then slow

sip of vodka milkshake,
three hours of vodka milkshakes

————————

      lady, stir
your vodka milkshake,
make it last, make it
unsludgy

————————

daffodils when Goldie Hawn
wants them—and Goldie
Hawn fades, she
likes to diminish in my eyes

————————

      slivovitz
Chanel at the Jewish
Museum

————————

Chanel belongs
in the Jewish Museum,
Marsden Hartley belongs in

the Rubin Museum of
Himalayan art

_____

    El Greco and
Milton Resnick nap and
take steam—

_____

flat ass of croupy man

_____

rumble seat spooning—
do you like to spoon?

_____

I speak too truthfully
about intimate matters
to strangers—but
Alice Notley says
"who reads poetry anyway!"

_____

    upper
lips are beauty repositories

_____

greedy for beauty, the upper
lip hogs the portion

_____

no moiety for upper lip,
it seizes and forecloses

_____

groove of my tongue in
your upper lip dent, upper
lip's divot or plumb line

_____

why are certain
intimate acts forbidden?

_____

if you have meningitis can
you get a meningitis shot or
is it too late?

_____

I always
fall in love with non-
reciprocators

_____

finding him hour after hour
in Sterling basement,
early nightmare john

_____

when did I begin dreaming
about public bathrooms crowded
with hobos grooming
themselves in mirrors?

_____

bird
thrum in background
achieves impersonality

_____

Odysseus
crossing dark lot to reach

Christmas department store
on drunk midnight

———————

addiction to
varieties of yellow
experience

———————

cook pork loin in law school
milk like Shirley Temple
who died this month

———————

    and then nerd
transformed into Ashley
Wilkes curls for me

———————

gently seduced by consent
in neighbor house,
his law-school neck explored

———————

shirtless
butcher-son with underage
Artforum columnist manqué

———————

dotage
in air-conditioned
hotel and AA talk show
Liza lesions

———————

I remember your appearance
on *Good Morning America*,
Charles Olson

———————

cover
photo of Ginsberg's cum—
cum smells like heroin

———————

meretricious
Goethe's guilty
fall into salumeria

———————

    sauerbraten
or Salomé's fatigue

———————

audition for fig compote

———————

will you qualify for one
filament of prune?

———————

legendary Mitropoulos,
Bernstein's mentor stroking
hung poetries

———————

    again Nagasaki
Sigmund Freud or Herbert
(George?) *Kismet*
Kiss Me, Kate? Sigmund
Romberg? *Die tote Stadt*?

———————

cult figure of Norma
child-murder?

———————

    trench mouth
trench warfare? homo
gestation in mustard gas—

———————

henceforth opera-pink
amnesiac vagabondage
dominates

———————

    rickety
traveler and his girl hip
overpraised despite
pork loin coagulation

———————

    decorator syphilis

———————

Poppins banister slide

————————

           use Yiddish
frequently in *Adonais* rewrite

————————

write recitative for his homo-
phobia opera buffa

————————

          envy
of his large eyes and
large pectorals, flabby
withal

————————

         cerebrum lid
removed and frozen,
five inches remaining matter

————————

        hieroglyph
cornholing in dawn omnibus

————————

extra-credit bellhop
hemorrhoid

————————

hagiography (omphalos?)
of Brigitte Bardot
quoted as surrendering

————————

      even if the phrase
fills me with panic

————————

sitting beside his disease
on bench, deciding not to
be disease but expel it

————————

and then receive imaginary
cure at meat counter
from butcher who lacks a shadow

Trance Notebook #29

[shopworn Cassandra towels
in requiem half-moon]

we lie rotting in fluid and
repeatedly mention
our cesspool identity

_____

she understood
I'm capable of growing
a beard

_____

this fluidity
diseased or
counterproductive

_____

am I culprit
for my own claustrophobia?

_____

unintentionally anti-Semitic
description of me as mouse

———————

sore throat
from solvents, not from
cadmium, unless Naples
yellow contains
unmarked cadmium

———————

eternal flames in
other people's nuclear
families, no eternal
flame in mine

———————

all-night
fruit-eating binge in Tapei

———————

he is now my
nude model in the
fictional sense of "now"
and "nude"

———————

morals
charges against Adam
and Eve for
shedding fig leaves

———————

God's undeniable horniness
evidenced by brief chapters
in Genesis

———————

her pregnancy
as a brief chapter in
Mercedes McCambridge

———————

starring
in Genesis as
Erda, Queen Mother
of Nothingness

———————

it stresses me out to talk
about Kinsey

————

    a tiny bottle
of egg shampoo in the mid-
1970s as Shakespeare
equivalent

————

dreaming of new uses for
rutabaga in Alice
Waters's living room

————

        there are no
new uses for rutabaga

————

he bites his cheeks and asks
hostile underconfident questions
about hormonal surges and
interrupted minimalism

————

National Book
Death Day, a day for
books to die

————————

we like to watch the death
of a book

————————

taking falling for granted

————————

philosophical dimensions of
51 ways to fall slowly

————————

unattached people like
Vicki falling

————————

       rejection of
Vicki and she falls

————————

         she
falls philosophically as
an "other" or a "compared" thing

————————

a long conversation with
Pallas Athena

───────

you suck he said to Mom,
who pretended to ignore
a son's *you suck*
on smartphone

───────

         apologize
to Cassandra

───────

         did your
parents understand the
significance of
slightly shopworn
Cassandra towels in
requiem half-moon?

───────

talc to ease the chafe

───────

an ear
for diphthong

―――――

lost Yiddish
phrase that sounds like "Midlothian"—
google Yiddish + Midlothian,
thereby find a Baltic state

―――――

gumbo
Elliott Gould
goulash
of rime and sea wrack

―――――

two nude bodies as Duras
asparagus urge

―――――

vertical
hold problem in *Villette*

―――――

laughter in honeymoon suite,
micropenis-flabbergasted bride

————————

    in
memoir a repeated
micropenis is
songful and funny

————————

    at dinner
parties stop
bragging about my big dong
and a dad
in white-collar prison

————————

    fatigue of thirty
women humming in the
Guggenheim rotunda

————————

is Adam Levine the second
sexiest man alive if I
am the first?

————————

it didn't faze the super
when I shoved my face
in his ass while he
kneeled to fix my toilet

————————

overdetermined
mutilations in Tennessee
Williams, surgery a symbol

————————

refusal to write about Tilda
Swinton sobbing into phone

————————

mother says my
heart's in storage

————————

lobotomy
bumps on back of neck

————————

Allen authorized
Naomi's lobotomy

_____

certain hooded French
lids I know, therefore diminution
lid, brevity lid

_____

    this gentleman
gave me a ride on his lap and I
cried while riding

_____

    drunken
bendable straight men
in Balthazar restroom

_____

at Brooklyn Thugs, a
weekly sex party, we
congregate for rapprochement
in lap dance and penetration

_____

I won't let you suck my cock
because you treated me in
racist fashion at the hardware store

_____

reject his anus permanently
because of its fetal or
Cain shadow

_____

Esau
shadow of his rejected
anus not a viable rhetoric

_____

pucker rose
he said on blog and I
blessed his nomenclature

_____

two
fingers he mistook for
painter phallus

_____

shame reading *Gourmet*
compulsively outside
Baltimore laundromat

_____

being told he is a
bad writer and believing it
in Jersey near cracked red oaks

_____

waiting for orange truth,
yellow truth, tetanus

_____

persuasive elm or
ember lyricism,
the long-dismantled ass

_____

an Emerson TV saved my
mother's life in 1955

_____

she took a bus to
Lucky Supermarket

———————

diced or sliced
pig's ears wrapped in impressive
lettuce leaves

———————

I flubbed that note
in the Fauré *Requiem*

———————

animals are more
flavorful when you
ignore their origins

Trance Notebook #30

[dribble cloth disguised as fashion statement]

      stepping
for hours into fugue states,
forgiving oneself for falling
into fugue

———————

      Sephardic
Jews who loved dates and
figs like international TV
stars in Newark and China

———————

the history of rice is the
history of vaudeville

———————

      small sticky
fragile words
gummed together

———————

narrative hammered out
on your own skin

_____

          porcelain
as exotic emblem

_____

      always accusing
me of barnyard stench

_____

mentioning butt-
fucking with surgical
lightness to escape *assoupir*

_____

      why try to
decide whether a certain
aesthetic act is evil?

_____

Wittgenstein addicts
pause but I don't pause

————————

am dreaming of negligees,
difference between negligees
and turpentine

————————

    —"flipping the
birdie"—

————————

      a nuance
fell into my gums between
two avoidable rainstorms

————————

we hired a guy
to lie flat in the tub—
my husband pissed
on him and then I screwed
my husband while the hired
guy watched

————————

nepotism makes me male—
I don't begin male,
I need to become male

————————

white
kerchief around my neck
is dribble cloth disguised
as fashion statement

————————

white kerchief in
back Levi's pocket signifies
a preference for what
shady sex act?

————————

cashiering in porn
theaters we encountered
shadows cast by voluptuaries

————————

we decided to
ruin our bodies as a way of entering
the novelistic

————————

    we didn't
sweat when we entered
the novelistic—we didn't
frame it formally as an entrance

————————

         a flashlight
reveals his rear tunnel's
figures and fissures—
Les Eyzies cave
paintings

————————

he will understand the
ass only when I explain
it to him

————————

explanation becomes
the ceremony's frame

————————

we end the ceremony
by smacking him

———

　　we count
holes on the belt
near the wading pool
and trellis at dawn,
up early so mother
and sister don't see—
a fantasy we entered
metrically

———

　　Alexander
Pope's shortness
bestowing the vagina
with a hut's omniscience

———

I've never known you to
be so promiscuous, he
said Glenn Gould said

———

　　honeymoon
shattered by deliberate

perverse abstinence though my
dick received honorable mention

_____

prefering sexuality to flee
the known—surprise
invasion from a source
formerly believed to be cold

_____

lipsmack
of Antony and Cleopatra drinking
wine in whirlpool

_____

considering
adolescence a cocktail
tidbit or a non-mistake
beside a pink building

_____

freshet of air the assertion
that mind differs from meat

_____

a small tube of
Vaseline an Egyptian
necessity you bring
into the afterworld, a permanent
hotel without electricity

———————

father distant from
gay son finds
remedy

———————

he enters the son's bedroom
and parts the quilted sea
to discover magnanimous
Acheron

———————

son's baccalaureate
in father's mouth

———————

Robert Redford's
opinion about Lautréamont

and Huysmans, fathers
huddled in my room

———————

      backseat
sodomy to the tune
of "Summer Breeze"—
we called it alcoholism
and sour fruit, we baked it

———————

he was a taut son,
verminous, envious

———————

      as his erotic
accomplice I was
feckless in Haifa
and lethargic like
grilled lobster
or melancholy
Jaques, the "k" a
forced cohabitation

———————

scapegoat
clairvoyance
turns danger
into candied kumquat

———————

the moment my father's
life ends
I might not witness

———————

afterward
who will forgive me
for dishonorable interior travel?

Trance Notebook #31

[like a camp counselor or a hurricane]

        lunch in Berlin,
hostility plus apologies

_____

contemporary ashamed
Germans give me apologies,
admiration and then
repeated ruthlessness,
can't help shaming me,
considering me risible and
small

_____

he didn't squeal with
enthusiasm when I
pointed my penis at him

_____

whom I perhaps have
shocked with my explicitness

————————

I always assume the
agenda is sexual and
it rarely is

————————

unaccountably he offers
shadow and protection
to me, like a camp
counselor or a hurricane

————————

permanent harbor, as
in original pizza
parlor sightings, or
older pianists melting

————————

affection
arrives as shock
and totality

————————

its omniscience
covers me up entirely,
repeals accident

_____

his vanishing
doesn't matter to me
factually, only symbolically

_____

all-consuming
symbolic eroticism like
a Turner sunset or
Whistler nocturne

_____

totality deserves
a hearing

_____

approach totality by
choosing a focus
for orgasms

_____

consommé
on New Year's Eve
and his AIDS death and
she vomits after we
have sex, completely
unsatisfying, not
one clue about female
anatomy or tempo—

———————

I think he
is a Jew, stapled
forced voice from damaged
larynx

———————

he bit the tip of my penis
in Boston, really hairy but
vile

———————

finger the cousin's balls
after his divorce, take a
lithography or etching lesson
from the police

————

grandparents weren't evil
but I was afraid of them

————

Schubert suffered from
analogical thinking, A & B
connected by Bridge of
Sighs

————

    plaisir d'amour
connecting diapers and choir

————

the Donner Party cannibalism boner

————

      the impossible
to resist Dad boner

————

a Goethe scholar in the
fog boner

————

any eye contact between
men is gay

———————

we eschew
eventfulness as an American
military strategy

———————

we
hate progress and
distrust national narratives

———————

an argument about rigidity,
a tragedienne's
falsetto

———————

an argument
about Medusa

———————

boner raga drone,
Tibetan stillness

————————

get
back to Noah's nudity

————————

Al
Jolson's heretical boner,
bad faith

————————

dream
of tiled floor in basement
barbershop—original glorious
violation—kid loses virginity
to barber

————————

which
barber? any barber

————————

Einstein's alleged nerdiness
also a boner

————————

don't try to pretend
that ultimatums (however
logical in tone) are reasoned
overtures

—————

he mentions
Poe in a dream

—————

wondering if momentariness
is a door

—————

mystery surrounding doors

—————

are pauses incidental?

—————

did she remove
objects that stained her
beauty?

—————

        Mandela's
tear ducts dried up, years
of limestone quarry

_____

and then this redness
appears as antidote or
lunatic contrast

_____

as in the repeated dream
when I renounce control
and see his red pants as
the answer to prayer

_____

       one Alex obscured
by a red flower

_____

stoned or
stunned flower

_____

without
trying, the flower has razor
burn, and we investigate

————————

my grandmother on
the terrace of containment,
honey I identify

————————

là ci
darem she hallucinated

————————

the catalyst of shame is
rage in action

————————

the trumpet's divinity
effaces Adam's and Noah's
postponed travel—

————————

the barber confessed that a
Jewish man (teacher)
molested him though
Judaism wasn't the cause

_____

    if we
believe in fatigue and
interpretation and a stinging
tribunal, a truncated
life and epiphanic
peepholes

_____

[clamor very is]
crossed out not because
I don't like it but
crossed out because
"clamor very is" is
not sensible

Trance Notebook #32

[blow job cut through with lime tenderness]

I
let my plant die—

_____

how much
soil and water does a
house plant need?

_____

his mother lived in
Elgin Marbles, a high rise
on a dry beach, and he
got over his depression to
become a better station
wagon driver

_____

the Coney Island
Petula Clark

_____

clamp clamp clamp—
why is *clamp*
important?

—————

we don't consider clarity
or sexual favors the goal

—————

    simply pressing,
pressing repeatedly to
imitate mother

—————

    writing
inside mother's clamped-
down body, a hand
that knows only how
to clamp

—————

he has a hot son and so
must violate the son
as a matter of policy
and martyrology

———————

a blow job cut through
with lime tenderness

———————

guilt and text and Shabbos
repudiate numbness

———————

we will die slowly and
no repair truck will arrive
to restore respiration

———————

in Israel she got sick,
maybe a bug, she lost
weight, it fed into her
compulsions

———————

I gave condolences in the
hospital elevator

———————

all
family closeness is
despicable, like the
son-in-law's aching
and clean request for
latkes

———————

and when
the irreproachably cute
one returns, we wonder
why they hid him down-
stairs, a sex and torture
business I operate
in the basement

———————

lubricated aggression,
speedy as a dead novel

———————

where will I
find all the penis photos
I need for my new expanded

dictionary of sexual
pleasure in the 19th
century?

_____

the clap is
a disease but also a
vigorously enthusiastic
response to a performance

_____

steady drinking
erodes my capacity to
appreciate gang
bang

_____

five minutes
of God

_____

she cut her
face as a God ethic

_____

a husband's mother
cut her face for God

———————

a male doula who
experiments on his own kids

———————

we'll die soon,
his "Meditation" from *Thaïs*
trimmed by Buddhism

———————

a huge vomiting
dog needs a shaman in
World War II

———————

how do we survive
World War III?

———————

a bandaged
continent

———————

neo-liberal
capitalism as tepid alterna-
tive to perpetual "cute"
warfare

———————

on Google Earth I saw
an old flame's house,
Maple Avenue

———————

the Y
chromosome is (like
cadmium orange or
angry men) a toxic
proposition

———————

little girl
takes off coat, holds bouquet,
obedient skirt glossy
yet stained

———————

doctor asks *have you seen
other penises?*

_____

Louis Waldon, star
of *Blue Movie,* is dead

_____

impulsive career of an
assassin's bullet, the
wet and inappropriate kiss

_____

a floppy LP free at
Safeway with purchase of
Funk & Wagnalls encyclopedia

_____

Mozart's
boyish beanie

_____

evil blue
lips on penguin,
6:45 hallucination

———————

teacher answers door in
bathrobe—a seen
butt, a birthday butt

———————

clinging
to birthday butt, hidden
brotherly cove

———————

genital mutilation, competence,
pitch in Jewish chanting,
penguin's magenta wings

———————

the butt factor's monotone

———————

nightmare
carpe diem, Hocquenghem
encore, circumcision
a controversial coronation

———————

death to the offered one
and to the one who offers

—————

what is HIV to you?

—————

      a rim
job wrecks it

—————

is that voice the architecture
of doom or a violet?

—————

      a settled
approach or a flood?

—————

little girl eating dried
seaweed as snack
is a good omen

Trance Notebook #33

[I decided not to keep up with the death drive]

shaving the private, shaving
the colonel

_____

offering walnuts to a stranger,
a jogger

_____

      peach
shard to a jogger, epitome of
the death drive, a debate I'm not
part of

_____

      I decided not to
keep up with the death drive

_____

      please mention that you
saw my butt

———————

*here is
your liver* (and he touches my
liver), *your bowels, your heart*

———————

he heard my
urine splash

———————

maybe
get a few compliments in
exchange for my subordination

———————

Klee's
Tunisian period, stacked
landscapes

———————

let the video be the dance
between two squirts of glue

———————

Connie Francis not yet
explained

———————

catch up on barebacking
discourse, catch up on
futurity discourse, Marxist
keywords, the New Testament

———————

olives
appear mute

———————

enigmas
accumulate

———————

I'm using Daddy as a
figure of speech, like rain

———————

is Daddy a puddle,
a permanent detachment?

―――――

discovering I need glasses
in the truck

―――――

I've never forgotten
his big pencil

―――――

don't
kick his big pencil!

―――――

looking into adjacent
trucks to see if truckdrivers
wear glasses

―――――

eyeglass store is
triangular

―――――

rationalization his word for
childhood error

———————

turn off lights because I
don't want to see your
face when I talk to you

———————

pallor of
phobic who changed his name

———————

tater tots shame food,
Mrs. Paul's fish sticks

———————

skinny overtanned
damaged orphan, longing
to be a lesbian

———————

did she become a
lesbian? why not
say so?

———————

sloth and anger of large-breasted
male receptionist, his ingrained
depressiveness, end of
story

———————

no consolation in
the denouement

———————

read the next
sentence for consolation

———————

the wading pool
interrupting (with her nipple)
the weeping peacock?

———————

per-
mitting perpetual prurience, a
newfound vocation

———————

unfettered
and constant arousal

_____

blobs overlain with blue
violet—

_____

      or else develop the
violet blue

_____

pigment sticks, dripping—

_____

a wiggly little girl
close to tears

_____

    calm
down and make cookies,
spaghetti sauce, find it
normal to make spaghetti
sauce—leading to tears
and reparative brisket

―――――

brisket as symbol of opulent
culture and obsequies

―――――

cruel penises
a minor tributary

―――――

forced
immobility, ballerina paralysis,
instructions to overcome
paralysis

―――――

Blanche DuBois's later
years in the asylum,
lobotomy as reward
for exorbitant dreaming

―――――

tight ill-
fitting boots and a head cold—
it happens to Jewish boys,

they get wet noses in
early winter

———————

     reserve at Garibaldi's
tomb, pray for Garibaldi's
soul, Garibaldi's incest—
student stuck
with incest as a rewarding
topic

———————

—make the mayor
happy, kill yourself

———————

indentured servant of the
people of New York and their
queer future

———————

     Judy Garland's
queer future as a wiggling

paralyzed ballerina with
"E" caught in the brain,
like Schumann's "A"—

———————

    amazing plurality
of thin-penis Schumanns suddenly
cold to me on camping trips
when we share sleeping bags

———————

watching *Imitation of Life* for
slow kicks in the infirmary—

———————

    and this threnody,
like Nono's, over-extends its ring

———————

Wagnerian tumescence, Mommy
tumescence, his ass "ample
as a classic six"

———————

—thank you
for the prostate stimulation—
curled up like a suicide
at the art colony

———————

a laughing nimbus
of imprecation surrounding
the avoided suicide—

———————

permanent
hickey is a paradox, hickeys
are temporary

———————

decomposing a
litany by sucking its nipples

———————

triggering a depressive fit
by saying "miss you" non-
stop for 20 minutes

———————

finding "time" an impossible
concept

———

twinkling star over black
river's tabula rasa

———

—and he falls—

———

a soft alligator
was eating his arm
in Florida nightmare

———

dreamt
they drove me to a mountain
Kunsthalle

———

a Russian
roulette demonstration,
a "conjugal Marxist"

———————

*I want to visit a concentration
camp* my mother says,
a lopsided request

———————

a *da* word was
on the tip of my tongue—not
Dad or Daddy but
Dante dopamine dastardly
Destry Rides Again?

———————

   *Five Easy
Pieces* Harvard Square
Theater loss of consciousness?

———————

  and maybe a father is
prosaic but most sons would
like to have sex with their
fathers or some moments
of physical intimacy

———————

ask about the
barbershop

———————

a litany of
squelched *Traviatas*—
liquid seeming animate, a
husband at every table

———————

most
men are rumors, false
hypotheses

———————

remember "Alice" pronounced
in three syllables as German name

———————

making a pass at
anyone, no statute of
limitations—

———————

dark-haired man
with very smooth shave

———————

being near
dark-haired men
while they shave

———————

sitting on the
sink while he shaves

———————

admitting
an attachment to him and then
rejecting him without explaining
the snub

———————

continuity
is never paradise

———————

       when
we urinate we are
obeying the principle of
continuity

_____

a cookie or a synagogue,
a tall doll

_____

cadeaux morsels—

_____

shadowboxing
with the barber
to whom I say
please manipulate
my jailbait
spiritus mundi

Trance Notebook #34

[the word she picks for comfort, "hernia"]

she has a
problem beginning and ending
an activity, be it
cloacal or conversational

_____

spends
five hours gradually chewing

_____

his belly a hard
place, I fall into the
sentence but have no-claim
on the sentence

_____

and the larger book as antidote

_____

kingfisher cults

————————

            Judith Blegen's
only broadcast performance
as Juliet

————————

        did I dream about
red mountain?

————————

            rub off
is an invert procedure—
I am a fussy child

————————

four drops of coffee spilled
on Hush Puppies

————————

Henry James was proleptic
about reproductive media

————————

proleptic is a nutty word

—————

she is not a vegetable

—————

would it
be an error to use
a nude model who might
write about the experience?

—————

consecutiveness perhaps
is the problem

—————

why must
thought be consecutive?

—————

conceiving of stoplessness
as a fatiguing protocol

—————

if her head flops to the
side, if food gathers on
the side of her face

————————

       wish for a long
trek in ice

————————

Herzog's handlebar mustache

————————

joy in formation of eye-
brow and occipital
cavity, like conch or
Kennedy half dollar

————————

on walk, listened
to squirrels

————————

       am I
squirrel-like?

————————

       anti-
Semitism was and is a fact
and I shouldn't encourage it

————

clinging to language remnants,
clinging to Joan Baez

————

discovering
a pituitary gland's function

————

prep-
ositional phrases
speed discourse onward?

————

*—do you find
the vibe tolerable*? I
don't find the vibe
tolerable

————

way
better than God, more
composed

————

          sometimes a girl—
his hairy arms cloaked
by tight-fitting accidie

_____

anhedonia sweater

_____

          looking objectively
ruins development

_____

shiny hands place
themselves in a story
that persecutes shininess

_____

          to become
immune I must master
measurement

_____

I like your hair—
how often do you wash

your hair I mean your
character's hair?

_____

        because
of his untouchable
vagabondage issues

_____

Rick's shoes say hi—
read triumphal strains
in their breezy tendency
to repeat

_____

      his boxers
showing and can I
ask him about his red
boxers, agreeable
and stable undies?

_____

I sold my underwear
(cum-stained) for $35

on craigslist—
that was my gravy

—————

     his shoes intrinsically
an invitation—could I
lick his knee?

—————

bop according to Kerouac
means mistake

—————

     make use of
every medium and every
circumstance and every hour
even if despair seems more
logical

—————

     smoke gets in
whose eyes? debris
of 1944

—————

the limited life
of Nelson Mandela dead
at 95 is not a
limited life

———————

the Moldau,
my metaphor for orgasmic
entrance into revolutionary
convulsiveness

———————

thoughts take place in
the larynx, but my hand,
distractible, is not a larynx

———————

why
not impress cocks
on church pews?

———————

originally Irene Dunne
in *Roberta* was

alive, her death
suddenly

———————

one could in Liszt's
era also be a merely
competent improviser,
Mozart's time, too

———————

take photos of young
bearded poets in
bathrooms, develop
a series based on
olfactory adventure,
visible or audible

———————

   half-asleep
or waking from near
slumber I wrote line
after line in loose
iambic pentameter—

———————

the world in which I breathed my last was wrong
according to the mother I betrayed

———————

depending on the mother's breath we took

———————

to demonstrate a peril absolute

———————

      we had no absolutes, we were in debt

———————

I thought to break my vow, but broke instead
the lash

———————

      a cad infectiousness

———————

we adequately gay, we adequate

———————

received the flow, a welt, where studies flew

———————

he kept a bee and almost grasped a hive

———————

where commas thrived and I alas expired

———————

however amplitude expressed itself,
an ampersand's regret, a faceted

———————

her beauty not negation, not believed,
a semen appetite, a cramp

———————

     we broke a vow,
we kept on saying "broke a vow"

———————

     a hetero
similitude, like Abel Gance

———————

Napoleonic codes and hair, to leak
a method actor's charm

———————

Commendatore
interviewed a lapsed and anti-gay

———————

a phobic retroactive fit, to green
or violet a land, finale blue

———————

his breast a fathomless reprieve
his breast a fathomless decree

———————

a caul
tremendousness, not chance

———————

and if there were a woman, spoon, retreat

———————

hi Christmas hat, a hotel booking, thrush

———————

just foamy yellowish October must
that we, that ouch, a penis lesson book

————————

she taught the loaf to pee, it took three years

————————

è quando, c'est l'amour, I'm thinking hard

————————

      they came to me at noon,
the dads and listeners, the timepiece drool

————————

free what, free oxygen is medium,
a regulation fitness bureau pox

————————

if Alice listens to adjudicate

————————

Kent Brown is dead, he killed himself, a loan

————————

truth loaned truth particles to ever me,
to never me, a stricture habitat

————————

Christ thanks and *allez* thinks, his Avignon
a port-o-san retablo crux, his greaves

————————

her blank regime of wanting ankle balm

————————

and lava came to spend the night in worm

————————

she thrust the penis into parallax,
she thrust the penis into adamant

————————

how could the hole unform, a hero hole,
heroic opening to Mars, if moon
allows?

————————

crazed tetanus,
oblige remix, *noblesse* solfège, Tom Mix

————————

my mother's favorite word
is "hernia," her one consoling roost,

the word she picks for comfort, "hernia"—
why "hernia" is comforting, I'll know
when oranges wish surrendering were fair

_____

Perec's smashed protocol, glass modishness,
my *éventail*, enveloping demesnes

_____

a hand in butt crack, exploration Mies,
how Mies explored butt crack when misers queued

_____

a cackle folderol, blue motet splash

_____

Bayreuth
modalities in blue and fishnet puce

_____

Bev wore a truss? in Bev we trust? trust what?
who's lunar Bev? a large and spandex fate

_____

grassiness, desuetude, macabre—
or almost when macabre is happiness

———————

        New Year's Eve:
before midnight we see in posthumous haste
Jane Eyre and *Letter from an Unknown Woman*
to bring back Joan Fontaine, who died
two weeks ago in Carmel-by-the-Sea

———————

long ago my mother fell down
on the sidewalk outside
a corner gas station

———————

I remember the sound
of her cry as she fell
in sunny Carmel—

———————

inchoate shout, gurgle—

———————

the culpable pavement's
irregularity caused her fall

—————

we can blame the city,
my father, the Fates,
or we can blame no one

—————

I remain an indirect,
untimely investigator
of the gurgle and the cry

Acknowledgments

The author thanks the editors of the following publications (print and online), in which portions of this book, sometimes in different versions, appeared:

Academy of American Poets (Poem-a-Day): "Trance Notebook #2 [nerdy questions about exact pitch]"

Animal Shelter: "Trance Notebook #1 [I believe in ruin]"

Argos Poetry Calendar 2015: "Trance Notebook #5 ['father' a category almost leviathan]"

Ashbery Home School: "Trance Notebook #17 [the lake and the kink]"

Boston Review: "Trance Notebook #18 [desire demands specialization]"

Dazed: "Trance Notebook #14 [cut it up and then project it]"

Document: "Trance Notebook #3 [a testicle descends, but a lark ascends]"

Essay Press: "Trance Notebook #22 [ultramarine has a pocky charisma]"

Literary Hub: "Trance Notebook #21 [surreptitious nookie with a large astronaut]"

The Lifted Brow: "Trance Notebook #29 [shopworn Cassandra towels in requiem half-moon]"

Night Papers: "Trance Notebook #23 [alabaster concussive effect of stillbirth]"

Paradis: "Trance Notebook #16 [nights illuminated by imperishable clutter]"

PEN American Center Poetry Series: "Trance Notebook #15 [the opposite of Tupperware]"

The Volta: "Trance Notebook #4 [the table doesn't have genitals]"

Washington Square: "Trance Notebook #12 [fruit binge]"

Wayne Koestenbaum has published seventeen books of poetry, nonfiction, and fiction, including *Rhapsodies of a Repeat Offender*, *Jackie Under My Skin*, *Andy Warhol*, *Hotel Theory*, *Humiliation*, *Best-Selling Jewish Porn Films*, *The Anatomy of Harpo Marx*, and *My 1980s & Other Essays*. His study of opera, *The Queen's Throat*, was a National Book Critics Circle Award finalist in 1993. The first solo exhibition of his paintings took place at White Columns in New York City in 2012. He has written an opera libretto (Michael Daugherty's *Jackie O*), and published essays and poetry in *The Best American Essays*, *The Best American Poetry*, *The New York Times*, *The New Yorker*, *London Review of Books*, *Artforum*, *Harper's*, *The Believer*, *Süddeutsche Zeitung*, *Cabinet*, and many other periodicals and anthologies. He received a B.A. from Harvard, an M.A. from Johns Hopkins, and a Ph.D. from Princeton. He has taught at Yale, in the English department as well as in the School of Art's painting department, and is now a Distinguished Professor of English at the CUNY Graduate Center in New York City.

Nightboat Books

Nightboat Books, a nonprofit organization, seeks to develop audiences for writers whose work resists convention and transcends boundaries. We publish books rich with poignancy, intelligence, and risk. Please visit our website, www.nightboat.org, to learn about our titles and how you can support our future publications.

The following individuals have supported the publication of this book. We thank them for their generosity and commitment to the mission of Nightboat Books:

Elizabeth Motika
Benjamin Taylor

In addition, this book has been made possible, in part, by grants from The Fund for Poetry, The National Endowment for the Arts, and The New York State Council on the Arts Literature Program.